MW00699534

Archie Bush

From Prairie to Philanthropy

Archie Bush

From Prairie to Philanthropy

Carl T. Narvestad

edited by Carol L. Heen, Ph.D.

NODIN PRESS

For permission to reproduce selections from this book and to learn more about Nodin Press, visit www.nodinpress.com.

ACKNOWLEDGMENTS
With thanks and appreciation for their efforts:Jennifer Alstad, Barb and Paul Benson, The Bush Foundation, Kari Ruth, Vivian Chow, *Granite Falls Advocate Tribune*, Granite Falls Historical Society, Terri Dinesen and Mary Gillespie, David Haroldson, Heen Century Digitization Project, Linda Heen, Leslie Heen, Margaret Holien, Elaine Johnson, Walter LaBatte, Maynard Museum, Gwen Jaenisch, Pioneer Public Televison, Shari Lamke and staff, Dave Smiglewski (Mayor of Granite Falls), Kris Swanson, Cathy Wurzer (Minnesota Public Radio), Yellow Medicine Historical Society, Megan Lipetzky, Norton Stillman, John Toren, and Nodin Press.

ISBN: 978-1-947237-53-7

Front cover photo, left to right: William McKnight, Guy Lombardo, Archue Bush. Courtesy Bush Foundation.

9 8 7 6 5 4 3 2 1

Library of Congress Control Number: 2023936757

Published by
Nodin Press
210 Edge Place
Minneapolis, MN   55418
www.nodinpress.com

Printed in U.S.A.

With thanks and appreciation to the hundreds of people,
then and now, who built Wang Township

Contents

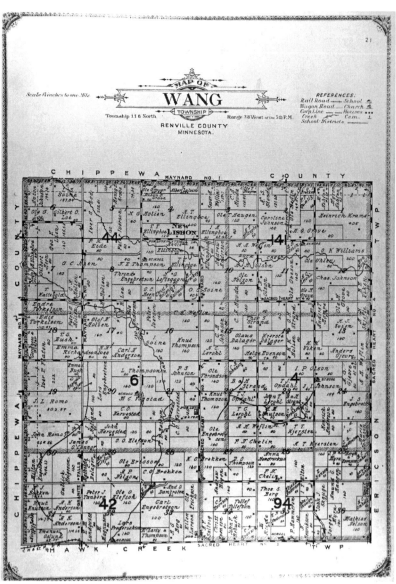

Wang Township, 1913

Preface and Editor's Notes

From where I am sitting, I can see the corner where Archie Bush was born in 1887, a little more than a mile away. I grew up hearing his story and I knew people who had been his childhood friends.

Carl Narvestad grew up knowing Archie's story even more completely. Carl's mother was a niece of Archie's stepmother. Carl spent his lifetime in the farm community of Wang Township, Renville County, Minnesota, living only a few miles from the Bush farm. Carl's mother and older sister Myrtle are among several people in a 1907 picture taken at the Tom and Emma Bush house after a meeting of the Vestre Sogn Church Ladies Aid. Archie's mother is on the porch, her hostess apron in place. His father is seated on the lawn along with a few other neighbor men, the minister, and the children. Sadie, Archie's older sister, is on the left. Many of my family members, including my great-grandmother, her sisters-in-law, and many neighbors, are there, too. Several of them had sailed on the same ship with Archie's mother, Emma, to America in 1866.

It is 2022, 115 years after that picture was taken. Carl, who spent more than a dozen years working on a biography of Archie Bush, knew the importance of his subject's life in business and philanthropy. When Carl died in 2003 at age eighty-eight, he left the twelve-chapter manuscript among his papers, and I happened upon it in 2019 while researching another topic at the Granite Falls Historical Society.

After finishing college at the University of Minnesota, Carl wrote professionally and never stopped writing, even after he took over the family farm. He and his dynamic wife, Amy Reinertson Narvestad, a former newspaper publisher and editor, were authors of at least fourteen books, including an 800-page centennial history of Yellow Medicine County and a biography of the pioneering tuberculosis physician, Dr. Kathleen Jordan.

Carl was a formidable researcher, finding original documents and interviewing people who were connected to the topic. He had an in-depth knowledge of the local area and environment. He knew the genealogy, geography, circumstances, setting, and values that influenced his subjects. For example, he interviewed one of his own high school classmates, who was a niece of Archie Bush, for the Bush biography.

Carl uncovered errors in previous reports and corrected them. For example, the Bush family moved to Minnesota in 1885, as shown by the

Minnesota census records, not 1887 as reported elsewhere. Carl examined birth records and proved that Archie Bush was born in Wang Township, Renville County, not the city of Granite Falls or Granite Falls Township. Carl determined the exact location of one of the Bush residences by interviewing neighbors, comparing distances and mileage locations. Carl confirmed that between 1895 and 1903 the Bush family lived on a rented farm in Section 36 of Granite Falls Township, east of the city of Granite Falls.

Much of Carl's lifelong writing was focused upon the Norwegian-American community. In recognition of his extraordinary work in Norwegian American history and culture, Carl was knighted in 1990 by King Olaf of Norway. In recognition of this honor, Carl was interviewed in his Minnesota home by Norwegian State Television.

The torch for local history carried by Carl has passed to me. In order to complete this biography, I have updated it with photos, maps, and additional research. Carl's overall organization for the book remains, but the first two chapters have new material. The other chapters have been edited throughout.

Archibald "Archie" Granville Bush
[photo courtey the Bush Foundation]

1

Archibald "Archie" Granville Bush

St. Paul, Minnesota, January 16, 1966, UPI—

Archibald G. Bush, Chairman of the Executive Committee of Minnesota Mining and Manufacturing [3M], died this morning at his winter home in Winter Park, Florida.

...reported in the *New York Times* obituaries and on page one of Minneapolis and St. Paul newspapers.

The prominent news of *Archibald* Bush's passing is an indication of the importance of his life. For fifty-seven years he had been a primary force in building 3M, a company of world impact. At the time of his death, Bush was 3M's executive vice president.

Throughout his career, Bush served on the boards of universities, banks, businesses, and other organizations. During his time with 3M he acquired a large personal fortune, established a major foundation, and became a generous philanthropist.

Archie Bush began his career with a four-month business education course in Duluth. He took a position as assistant bookkeeper for a new, struggling mining and sandpaper manufacturing company at a salary of $11.55 a week. He rode the ups and downs of the roller coaster years until the company reached its heights as Minnesota Mining and Manufacturing (3M).

Bush had traveled a long distance since his birth, March 5, 1887, on a prairie farm in Wang Township, Renville County, Minnesota. His early years on the farm and working within the farm community served him well for the challenges of his later life.

2

Birthplace and Parents

ARCHIE'S BIRTHPLACE: WANG TOWNSHIP, RENVILLE COUNTY, MINNESOTA

The vast prairie land of western Minnesota became part of the United States through the Louisiana Purchase in 1803. These miles of tall prairie grasses are interrupted only by the Minnesota River Valley and small lakes and creeks. Carved by an ancient glacier, the river valley, one mile across, was produced by the Glacial River Warren. Bedrock granite exposed by the glacier, among the oldest exposed rock on earth, was clearly visible in the valley.

The land was untouched tall-grass prairie until the 1860s. Native prairie grasses, growing as tall as six feet, have even deeper roots, and the soils had been enriched by the plants for thousands of years. The prairie was the home of the Dakota people and the buffalo herds on which they depended.

The Louisiana Purchase set off a series of

changes and events, beginning with the need to survey the vast prairie lands. Cartographers and surveyors began describing and delineating the uncharted areas of the Louisiana Purchase into numbered, thirty-six-square-mile townships, according to the dictates of the national Northwest Ordinance of 1787.

These cartographers and surveyors followed a rough trail, soon known as the Abercrombie Trail, which went from Ft. Snelling in eastern Minnesota, to the Dakota territory. The Abercrombie Trail was a main road, heavily used by expeditions, army troops, fur traders with two-wheel oxcarts, wagon trains headed for the Montana gold rush, and ultimately, by settlers and homesteaders. The trail cut diagonally across Wang township, cutting deep ruts that remained visible decades later, testifying to its constant use in the 1800's.

Meanwhile, The Dakota people who occupied the prairie were having their lands restricted and re-defined. In 1858, all the reservation land north of the Minnesota River was negotiated away for a modest price (most of which went unpaid), and the Dakota were confined to a long, narrow reservation on the south rim of the Minnesota River Valley, where the government set up two agencies known as the Upper and Lower Sioux Agencies.

By 1862, the conditions for the survival of the native people were dire. Their long-festering grievances exploded in August, leading to a war with hundreds of deaths and flights out of the counties. The final conflict, misnamed the Battle of Wood Lake, occurred on reservation land a few miles south of the Minnesota River valley, ten miles from the future Wang Township. As a result of the war, reservation land was reclaimed by the government, and the Native Americans were removed to camps.

The Federal government quickly made former reservation lands available for homesteading. Within five years the first homesteaders arrived for claims and began giving names to the numbered townships. Local township governments were formed and township officers were elected.

Minnesota Township #116, Range 38, was settled rapidly by Norwegian immigrants. In 1875, Wang Township was officially organized and named in honor of the Vang, Valdres, district of Norway. The settlers carried with them their Norwegian customs, language, religion and traditions. The immigrants homesteaded land, established churches, and built schools in their new township.

Some of the first homesteaders in Wang Township were five Norwegian families from the Oslo area. They arrived in Wang Township in 1867, having made the trip from Fillmore County, Minnesota, in ox-drawn wagons. In 1871, only six years after the Dakota Conflict ended, the next major influx of immigrants (more than thirty fam-

The Minnesota River Valley today, four miles south of the Bush farm, near Granite Falls

ilies) arrived from Vang, Valdres, Norway. More neighbors and relatives from the Valdres Valley soon followed. A local post office, called New Lisbon, began operating in Wang Township, Section 4, in the home of A. T. Ellingboe. Very few towns sprang up before the appearance of the railroads in the 1880's.

The Wang homesteaders conversed in the Valdres dialect, which was distinct from other Norwegian speech. Children spoke only Norwegian until they began learning English in school. During recess, children played Norwegian games such as "jeppe pinne" and called to each other in their first language, Norwegian.

The children attended "parochial school" for one month each year. These sessions were part of the Norwegian Lutheran Church practices. In Wang Township, three Norwegian Lutheran Churches were founded, two miles apart from each other. All church proceedings, religion instruction, and parochial school were conducted in Norwegian. Following the Norwegian tradition, men sat on one side of the church and women and children sat on the other side during Sunday services. These Norwegian practices continued for decades.

By the mid-1870's, six country schools were operating in the township. Schools had eight grades and were attended by children as well as adult immigrants who wanted to learn English.

Soon all thirty-six square miles of Wang Township farmland were owned and occupied by homesteaders. Hundreds of people were farming, building homes, and expanding their families. Within two decades, more than five hundred people lived in the township.

The farmers were producing grain, which had to be brought to market. To serve the need for grain shipments, Wang Township residents build a new grain elevator at the south end of the township along the newly built railroad line. Railroads were extending their lines to the west and constructing depots, around which towns would be built. The towns that developed near Wang Township were Maynard, Sacred Heart, and Granite Falls.

Wang Township was the future home of the Bush family, and the birthplace of Archibald G. Bush.

ARCHIE'S MOTHER:
EMMA HAMRE RICHARDSON BUSH

All of Archie's maternal ancestors were from the Valdres Valley of south central Norway. Sometimes called "The Queen of the Valleys," Valdres Valley is home to many of Norway's wooden stave churches, still standing after a thousand years. The beautiful valley starts on the southern slopes of the mighty *Jotunheiman* (home of the giants) Mountains, Norway's most imposing range of snow-clad peaks. The valley descends southward some eighty miles.

However, nature's beauty does not translate into good farmland. The crop season is short and sometimes plants freeze before they are ripe. Mountainside fields are only an acre or two and every spear of grass needs to be harvested, usually by manual labor.

In the 1800's Valdres Valley farms were small and resources were few, but farm families were large. Beginning in the 1850's people began leaving the valley, with hopes of a better life in America.

The U. S. Homestead Act of 1862, and accompanying recruitment for new settlers, produced a large emigration from Norway in the mid 1860s and 1870s. Valdres lost a high percentage of population through emigration to America. Some people left behind parents and siblings; others traveled in extended family groups with many children. Ships' records show multiple generations

Maynard, Minnesota, Main Street, ca. 1880-90, the town closest to the Bush farm

of siblings, spouses, and children all sailing on the same vessel and headed for the same place.

The newly arrived immigrants often settled on adjacent farms. They shared work and customs, building a community with strong ties to Norwegian language and traditions. Archie Bush's mother was part of this world.

Emma Bush was born Ingeborg/Emma Hamre in 1848 in the Valdres Valley. Her mother was Marit Knutsdatter Fygle (1827-1890) and her father was sixteen-year old Amund Helgeson Hamre (1832-1923). The Fygle farm where Emma grew up was described as: "a very small farm. At one time it was the smallest farm in Vang, Valdres. It supported one cow and some smaller animals. It was situated so that the snow remained on the ground until late spring, often having large drifts until the last of May."

Ingeborg learned the meaning of struggle and poverty at an early age. At age eighteen, she decided to leave the struggle behind and join the wave of emigrants heading to America. On April 13, 1866, she officially signed out from the Vang Church in Valdres, leaving behind her mother, who was now married to Jorge Helgeson and was busy raising a new family. She also left behind her father, Amund Hamre, who was married to Dorte Lerhol and was also raising a family.

Twelve days later, on April 25, 1866, Ingeborg sailed from Bergen, Norway, to Quebec on the *Frederick Petersen*. She was not traveling alone. Of the 311 passengers on board for the six-week trip, about half of the passengers were Ingeborg's neighbors from the Valdres Valley. Many were family groups of parents and young children. Accompanying Ingeborg on the voyage was Thomas Kristofferson Lerhol, neighbor and distant relative.

Upon arriving in America, Ingeborg went to the Northfield/Goodhue County area of eastern Minnesota where her uncle, Jon Hamre, had settled in the 1850's. This area had become a Valdres Valley enclave. Ingeborg adopted the custom of Americanizing her name and became known as "Emma" Ingeborg Hamre. Direct evidence of her life during these early years is sketchy. According to her granddaughter, her first jobs included housework. It is believed that Emma visited her numerous relatives in Goodhue County before seeing other relatives and neighbors who were homesteading land in Wang Township, Renville County.

Like the Valdres settlement in Goodhue County, Wang Township was a Valdres settlement being established in western Minnesota. Between 1870 and 1875, at least thirty-three people from eleven households who were on the 1866 *Fredrick Petersen* voyage homesteaded farms in Wang Township. Among the settlers in this Norwegian Lutheran community was Thomas Lerohl, who had accompanied Ingeborg on the voyage to America. Eventually, both sides of Ingeborg's family emigrated to America to live among the same Valdres farm neighbors in Wang Township in Minnesota.

Little is known of Emma's first nine years in America. In 1875, she married William Richardson at Fort Buford, in far western Dakotah Territory. Richardson, born in Skirlaugh, Yorkshire, England in 1847, was an army druggist. He may have immigrated at age 24 in 1871 through Ontario, Canada, a common entry point for those bound for the mid-west. According to U. S. Army records, he enlisted on April 11, 1872, noting his place of birth and occupation as "druggist."

On February 20, 1876, William and Emma had their first child, a daughter, Sadie Ann. After Sadie, Emma and William had three more children.

On April 14, 1877, after five years with the army, Richardson re-enlisted at Fort Buford. Located near the Montana border, Ft. Buford was 22 miles south of present-day Williston at the confluence of the Missouri and Yellowstone Rivers. The fort was built in 1866 to protect the overland routes and the construction of rail lines into Montana Territory. (In 1881, the fort was the site of Sitting Bull's surrender, and by 1895 the fort was closed.)

In 1880, William Richardson died, although no gravesite has been located. It is possible the family was in Dakota or at Ft. Sill near Oklahoma City, Oklahoma Territory.

By 1882 Emma was at a crossroads. She had managed her own emigration, found work, married, and had four children. Her husband had died, as had three of the children. Once again on her own, she decided to build her own future. On June 6, 1882, two years after her husband's death, Emma Hamre Richardson bought 120 acres of farmland from Ole Akerland in Wang Township (the South Half of the Southeast Quarter of Section 18). With this decision she set the stage for the lives of her entire family.

Relatively few single women bought farmland in those years, but a farm offered a place to live and have income from crops. The Fygle farm in Norway where Emma was born had only 16 acres of cropable land; the remainder was timberland on the mountainside. With her purchase of 120 acres, and within two years 40 more acres, Emma owned ten times the amount of land as the Fygle farm. Her land was rich, flat, and tillable. She owned land totaling a quarter section, measuring half a mile by half a mile. Emma had made herself a landowner with opportunity ahead. The poverty of the Valdres Valley was far behind her. Her land on the prairie above the Minnesota River Valley offered prosperity through an investment of effort.

Although Emma now owned a farm, she did not immediately move back to Minnesota. She was living in Oklahoma with her one surviving child, Sadie. Her life changed when she met Thomas Granville Bush in 1883.

Archie's Father: Thomas Granville Bush

Thomas Granville Bush (1858–1951), had spent his first working years as a cattleman in Texas and Oklahoma. At age twenty-five, he married Emma/Ingeborg Hamre Richardson on October 1, 1883, at Fort Sill, Oklahoma.

Thomas Bush's early childhood had been lived in West Virginia. Born in 1858 at Tanner's Fork near Parkersburg, West Virginia, Thomas was the eldest child of Isaac (1835-1901) and Louisa Miner Bush (1834-1925). In 1866, when Thomas was eight, the family moved from the Appalachian region of West Virginia to northern Texas, near the Oklahoma border. Isaac and Louisa Bush lived in rural Grayson County, Texas, until their deaths, in 1901 and 1925.

After their marriage, Thomas and Emma lived in Texas where, on June 3, 1884, their first son, Reuben Bush, was born.

While living in Texas, Emma, now Emma Bush, continued to buy farmland in Minnesota. She purchased forty additional acres adjacent to her property in Wang Township, Renville County. Like her first purchase, the property had been homesteaded previously and required no proving of a claim. Emma owned 160 acres, a sizeable farm for Minnesota.

In 1885, Emma and Thomas Bush moved their family from Texas to Minnesota to begin farming Emma's land.

More than land awaited the Emma and Tom Bush family in Wang Township. The people of the farm community included many of Emma's relatives and neighbors from the Valdres Valley. This community embraced Emma's past in Norway and her future in America.

ARCHIE'S MATERNAL GRANDFATHER: AMUND HAMRE

When Emma left for America, she had left behind her father, Amund Hamre. Amund had married Dorte Lerhol in 1864, and by 1879 had six children. Amund did not have an easy life on his Valdres Valley farm. A niece of Amund's wife described the situation: "Everyone was poor but some were poorer than others. The Hamre's oldest son, Helge, would visit relatives and family friends and be given gifts of food so heavy that we all felt sorry for him having to carry such loads of food."

Helge decided to emigrate to America as his half-sister had done before him. In 1879 he arrived at the Norwegian immigrant community in Goodhue County, where Uncle Jon Hamre lived. From there, Helge traveled to western Minnesota and by 1881 was living just south of Wang Township in Granite Falls, Minnesota.

In 1881, Emma and Helge's father, Amund Hamre also emigrated, leaving his children and wife behind in Norway while he established a home for them in America. In 1882, Amund settled on a farm near his son, Helge, in Wang Township. Later that year, his wife and children joined him.

The Amund Hamre family bought an eighty-acre farm on May 9, 1885 (North Half of the Southeast Quarter of Section 18 and the Northeast Quarter of the Southwest Quarter of Section 19). This farm was adjacent to the land already owned by his daughter, Emma, but was only half the size.

When Emma Bush and her family arrived in Minnesota from Texas in 1885, she saw her father for the first time in nineteen years. During that time, she had married, had children, lost

children, been widowed, married again, and had
more children. Now, with her husband and children, she finally met her eight half-siblings, who
ranged in age from three to twenty-three years old.
The entire Hamre family lived only a few minutes'
walk from her home. She had an uncle, also named
Helge Hamre, living five miles away.

Emma was thirty-six. Nearly two decades had
passed since she arrived from Norway. She had
lived in Dakota Territory, Oklahoma, and Texas.
By moving to Wang Township, Emma was reunit-
ing with people from both sides of her family, as
well as friends and neighbors from Norway. This
community provided the values, language, religion,
and traditions in which Emma's children were
raised.

Many Norwegian families were reunited in
these years. Amund's wife, Dorte, saw her sister
Berte and brother-in-law Torstein Hoverstad for
the first time in twenty-three years. They were
neighbors once again. Dorte saw her brother
Thomas Lerhol for the first time in nineteen years.
Thomas, who had traveled with Emma on the voyage to America, lived nearby. Thomas and Emma
met again after nearly two decades.

Emma was also reunited with relatives from
her mother's family. Six of her Holien (Fygle) first
cousins, their father and his two older sons, were
farming just a few miles from her property.

Relatives and neighbors from Valdres Valley
were once again neighbors. They were living along

the Minnesota River Valley in Wang Township, working farm by farm and creating their futures together.

3

Early Years

THE BIRTH OF ARCHIBALD "ARCHIE" GRANVILLE BUSH

Two years after Emma and Thomas Bush arrived in Wang Township, they had their second son, Archibald Granville Bush. He was born on their farm on March 5, 1887. His half-sister, Sadie, was twelve years old and his brother, Reuben, was three years old. Soon Archie would have two additional sisters, Margaret Louise and Minnie Grace.

In 1887, the year of Archie's birth:

- Buffalo Bill was touring Europe
- The Dawes Act was passed
- George Abbott was born
- Eiffel started work on a tower
- Tesla and Edison were engaged in electricity experiments
- Verdi was writing his operas
- Anne Sullivan began teaching Helen Keller
- Van Gogh cut off his ear
- The US Constitution was 100 years old
- Grover Cleveland was president

- The first Sherlock Holmes stories were published
- Theodore Roosevelt lost many of his cattle in the great blizzard which ended his ranching days in North Dakota
- Sinclair Lewis, the author from Sauk Centre, Minnesota, who would become America's first Nobel Prize winner in literature, was two years old.
- Locally, in Granite Falls, Andrew Volstead was the county attorney. He was considering running for Congress.

Just north of Granite Falls, the Bush family was involved in school and church activities. Emma Bush was an active and faithful contributor to Vestre Sogn Lutheran Church, located two miles east of the Bush farm. Vestre Sogn ("West Parish") was the first church congregation established in Wang. The church building had been constructed in 1881.

Archie Bush, along with siblings Reuben and Margaret, was baptized at the nearby home of Mr. and Mrs. Endre Thorkelson, on May 27, 1890, according to the Wang Lutheran Church records. The godparents and sponsors were Helge H. Hamre, Else H. Hamre, Margaret H. Hamre and Helge A. Hamre (Emma's uncle and wife, and her brother and sister). In April 1895, three-year-old Minnie Grace Bush was baptized at Vestre Sogn Church.

Vestre Sogn Church interior, between 1882 and 1892, Wang Township, Section 21

The Bush family life was centered upon farming. Everyone had roles and responsibilities on the farm. Children had many daily tasks: horses and cattle were fed and watered, cows milked, chickens fed and eggs picked, hogs tended, harnesses repaired, teams hooked to implements, fields tilled, hay stacked, grain planted and harvested. The children were taught their chores by Tom and Emma, each of whom brought many skills to the farm life. Farming was a family effort.

Animals were butchered at home and meat was smoked. Bread was baked often. Drinking water was carried to the house, after being pumped by hand from a nearby well. Butter was churned, usually by the children. Light came from kerosene lanterns, and wood had to be chopped for use in the cookstove. Clothing was often home spun and hand sewn. A vegetable garden was a necessity. Infrequent trips were made to nearby towns for staples such as coffee and sugar. These trips to town were probably accomplished using a horse and buggy rather than the heavy draft workhorses used for farm work.

Between school and farm chores, Archie had little time for play. One of his work tasks was to weed the garden. Of all the farm chores, this was the job he most disliked. One day he persuaded his mother to let him go fishing at nearby Hawk Creek instead of weeding. Hawk Creek was the local swimming hole during the summer and the

Granite Falls Main Street

ice skating site in the winter. It also abounded with game fish. Archie promised to bring home fish for supper, but that day fishing was poor. All Archie caught was one six-inch bullhead.

In addition to Hawk Creek, there were also large wetlands known as "sloughs." One of these wetlands, known as the Hoverstad slough, was a mile long and was located just across the road from the Bush farm. The slough was dotted with muskrat houses, and trapping muskrats was comparatively simple. Archie learned to trap and skin muskrats from a neighbor boy, Christopher N. Holien, who later recalled that "little Archie" liked to go along in hopes of selling a pelt for ten cents. These dimes were the first money Archie earned for himself.

Childhood was a mixture of church, school, nature, work, play, and adventures. Young Archie showed a boyish spirit of determination, according to a story in the *3M Megaphone* in 1959. "One day playing in the yard of his home he announced he was going to grab that eight-month-old bull by the head and throw him down. As he approached the bull, it showed no concern for this threat to his peaceful grazing. Even when the young 'cowboy' grabbed the bull's head and started twisting, the animal showed no alarm. Such lack of response was a blow to Archie's ego. He became angry and screamed, "If I can't throw you, I'll ride you." He scrambled onto the bull's back. This transformed the animal's character—pitching and kicking, the bull tossed his youthful rider into a nearby mud puddle...soft mud. Little Archie was unhurt but temporarily defeated."

The *Megaphone* continued with a story about Archie's horsemanship—or lack thereof. One of Archie's attempts to secretly ride a mare resulted in young Archie hanging onto the saddle horn and screaming at the top of his lungs as the horse galloped across the yard. Archie dismounted—head-first. Archie's father, Thomas Granville Bush, had been a cowboy in Texas and Oklahoma and recognized his son's apparent lack of or undeveloped ability with horses.

By June of 1895, when Archie was eight, the Bushes moved to a rented farm three miles away, near the village of Granite Falls. The Minnesota State census recorded them living in section 36 of Granite Falls Township: Thomas G. Bush 38,

Emma 46, Sarah (Sadie) Richardson 19, Reuben 10, Archibald 8, Margaret 7, and Millie (sp) 3. According to the 1900 federal census, they were still living at this location. This farm home was close to the village and its school, and to the homes of Emma's Holien-Fygle cousins and other Hamre families. The Bush family lived on this farm for eight years. There is no information about who was farming Emma's acreage during this time.

The family returned to their Wang Township farm in 1903. A large house had been constructed on Emma's land and was ready for them when they moved back and resumed farming. (On a bedroom window of the new Bush home, young Archie Bush etched his name in the glass. This etching was observed in the 1950's by then tenant, Margaret Holien.) Tom Bush bought his father-in-law's 80 acres of land, bringing the Bush property to a total of 240 acres.

A photo taken in 1907 shows the Bush farmhouse during a meeting of the Ladies Aid Society of Vestre Sogn Church. Emma Bush and daughter, Sadie Richardson, are there, surrounded by many friends and neighbors from both Norway and Minnesota. Tom Bush is there, too, seated on the grass with the minister and neighbors.

School and a Good Student

When the Bush children started attending school in the 1890's, Wang Township had six one-room

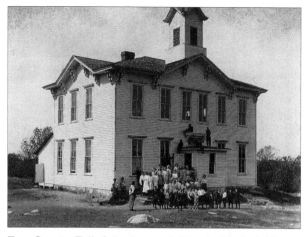

East Granite Falls School, attended by the Bush children

country schools. In 1895, after the family moved near Granite Falls, Archie and his siblings attended the East Granite Falls school. They walked the three miles to and from school, rode horseback, or occasionally took the family buggy.

Archie was a good student and became the favorite of one of his teachers. Occasionally, he would give the instructor an argument if he did not agree. One teacher thought this showed "spirit."

The *3M Megaphone* reports: "In school, his activities were like those of any boy—study, games, parties and fights. Usually, he was organizing the games and parties; he preferred to lead, not to follow. In the art of self-defense, he was able to take care of himself when the occasion arose."

Upon graduation from East Granite Falls High School, Archie gave some thought to becoming a teacher. During the winter months he

The Thomas and Emma Bush Family, ca. 1909. Archie is at the far left in the back row.

attended special classes in town, passed an examination, and qualified as a teacher. However, his interest waned upon realizing that country schoolteachers were earning only $40 a month.

Archie learned to play the fiddle, probably taught by his uncle Thomas Hamre. Thomas was a talented country fiddler and had learned to "make-do" if needed. When confronted by a bow with loose string, he wound the bow hair around his finger and played while others danced.

With an early eye to income, teenage Archie picked up an extra three or four dollars on Saturday nights as manager of a three-piece band in Maynard, the nearest town to the Wang farm. His brother Reuben Bush played the violin and was probably part of the three-piece dance orchestra. At dances, Archie was in demand as a floor manager and caller for square dances and quadrilles. His strong, deep voice was often heard over the strains of the fiddles calling, "Allemande left and grand right and left. When you get your partner what'll you do? You'll swing her and she'll swing you."

It was also said that Archie, open to the opportunity to make a few dollars, managed a Maynard baseball team. It may be that he managed the team, but a village of some two to three hundred population would probably have difficulty finding cash for buying balls, so Archie perhaps volunteered his services.

Archie's farm days ended in 1908 when he was twenty-one. His neighbors remembered him as a happy farmer because they could hear him whistling while he made the rounds in the fields, according to Ruth Slattum in a conversation with Les Heen. Though he was a hard worker, he was laid low in haying and harvest time by hay fever. Perhaps this was why his father once told him he was "worthless." At any rate Archie knew where the air would be good for his ailment—on the shores of Lake Superior. He went north to begin a new life.

Tom and Emma Bush remained on the farm in Wang Township for only five more years, until 1913. By then, all the children were grown and making their own lives. After twenty-eight years on farms, Emma and Tom moved into the town of Granite Falls permanently.

By then the long-abandoned Abercrombie Trail had melted into ruts in the fields near Emma's farm.

4

The Beginnings of 3M: Minnesota Mining and Manufacturing

Northern Minnesota was home to the rich, highly productive Vermilion and Mesabi iron ranges. Geologists, prospectors, and average citizens avidly searched for the next big mineral strike. The discovery of a new ore, whether iron, copper, or another type, might produce the next bonanza for a lucky owner or investor.

In 1901, on the north shore of Lake Superior near Two Harbors, a new deposit of "corundum" was discovered. Corundum was a hard, course ore that was an ingredient in the making of abrasives, and this was the first corundum deposit found in the United States. Such abrasives were used for polishing and smoothing surfaces as well as in the production of grinding wheels and sandpaper. In recent years, the industrial demand for abrasives had grown rapidly. Discovery of a corundum deposit within the United States had great potential.

News of this corundum discovery spread throughout the community. Imagining the seemingly limitless mineral deposits, five local businessmen decided to form a company: Henry S. Bryan (owner of the ore property), Dr. J. Danley Budd, Herman Cable, William A. McGonagle, and John Dwan. On July 15, 1902, they created Minnesota Mining and Manufacturing, Inc.

The Minnesota Mining and Manufacturing Articles of Incorporation were not limited to mining corundum. The articles included: "quarrying, crushing, analyzing, smelting, shipping and marketing abrasives of all kinds and other mineral products." The inclusion of this clause would prove important in the years ahead.

At the 1903 annual meeting of Minnesota Mining and Manufacturing, the investors set a goal for ore production and shipping by that fall. They built a six-story building, dock, and housing near the Crystal Bay mine. Orders were placed for heavy mining equipment and machinery.

On January 21, 1904, Herman Cable was able to report that the test sample of corundum seemed satisfactory. The first sale of ore was made in March and 4,400 pounds of the product were ready to be sold and shipped. The investors were hopeful.

The investors didn't know that the first sale of corundum was to be the last. The ore, which initially looked so promising, was, in fact, much inferior to other abrasive materials which were being imported. Over the next few months, the disappointing quality of the corundum ore became apparent. No one was buying the ore for use as an abrasive. In fact, the ore was not actually corundum, a vital point not understood by the company for some years. The deposit had been wrongly identified; it was actually a low grade anorthosite and was not suitable as an abrasive. Years of planning, money, and effort were invested before this ugly truth fully emerged.

With no ore sales, salaries went unpaid. Creditors pressed for resolution. The officers endeavored to save their company "By the end of 1904", according to the 3M company history, *Brand of the Tartan.* "3M stock had dropped to an all-time low in the barroom exchange—two shares for a shot, and cheap whiskey at that."

Fortunately, two St. Paul investors, Edgar Ober and Lucious Pond Ordway, added their input and capital. Ordway's idea was to turn the company focus away from shipping ore to manufacturing grinding wheels and sandpaper.

By May of 1905, the direction of the company had changed. It was reducing its efforts at the Crystal Bay mine and moving into manufacturing. The *Duluth News Tribune* reported, "E. B. Ober, L.P. Ordway and D.D. Smith of St. Paul have secured control of 3M…and under the new management the company proposes to spend $100,000 in Duluth for the manufacture of sandpaper, emery wheels and other abrasive products." The company renovated the old Imperial Flour building in Duluth for its new manufacturing plant.

The next challenge that confronted the firm was provided by Mother Nature. On November 28, 1905, a major winter storm washed the company's mining warehouse, its contents, the ore, and the dock into Lake Superior.

Fortunately, by January 1906, the company was operating its Duluth manufacturing plant. Abrasive products were being produced for sale to furniture factories, shoemakers, carriage builders, sash and door factories and hardware stores. Mining diminished as manufacturing increased in the operation of Minnesota Mining and Manufacturing.

However, the company expenses still exceeded income. The investors had to secure loans outside their resources. Then came the financial Panic of 1907. The young company held on to customers by price-cutting.

Despite the financial pressures, the company needed staff. In 1907, they hired an assistant bookkeeper: William Lester McKnight. A twenty-year-old redheaded farm boy from White, South Dakota, McKnight had been going to school at Duluth Business University. McKnight soon came up with innovative ideas about running the company. His ideas caught the attention of management, and his work expanded into cost accounting in 1909. After two more years in this role in the Minnesota home office, McKnight was promoted to office manager and transferred to the Chicago sales office.

When McKnight was promoted in 1909, the company again needed an assistant bookkeeper. The twenty-two–year old man who appeared for the job was Archibald Granville Bush. Like McKnight, Bush's starting salary was $11.55 per week. Bush had been in Duluth for a year, building docks for two dollars a day while saving money for school. In January of 1909 he was enrolled in Duluth Business University. By taking evening classes, he finished the six-month course in four months and immediately went to work at Minnesota Mining and Manufacturing.

From *Brand of the Tartan*: "A.G. Bush was the opposite of McKnight both in appearance and personality. He was an athletic-appearing young man, 5'10", with straight blond hair, blue eyes, a light complexion which always had the 'just scrubbed' look of a small boy ready for church. He mixed well with all people and liked to keep on the go; his energy seemed limitless and he was unusually impatient with slowness in others."

Four months after Bush joined the company, when McKnight was promoted, Bush was promoted to the head bookkeeping position. As McKnight advanced within the company, so did Bush.

McKnight and Bush were born eight months and eighty-four miles apart. The two men, both raised on farms, became friends at the beginning of their careers and were colleagues for the rest of their lives. Together they put their stamp on the company.

In 1910, the company moved to a new home in St. Paul Minnesota, where it remained and from which it expanded. McKnight and Bush moved with the business and became part of the expansion.

5

Archie Bush Moves to St. Paul, Boston, Chicago

When McKnight and Bush joined the young Minnesota Mining and Manufacturing company, the business was struggling. Problems included operating capital, debts, lack of sales, and poor quality control. The damp conditions in Duluth hindered the successful drying of the sandpaper adhesive. By moving production from Duluth to St. Paul in 1910, this issue was partially solved. Meanwhile, some of the original investors elected to focus on their other obligations. As a result, financing, operations, and sales underwent critical changes. Staffing and job responsibilities also changed.

One of Bush's new responsibilities was inventory at the new St. Paul plant. Bush and a fellow-worker named Hull organized and counted the bags of raw materials—garnet, flint, and "corundum." After neatly stacking the hundred-pound bags in the center of the factory floor, they went home for the evening. The excessive weight in the middle of the floor proved to be too much for the structure. The floor collapsed, sending all the bags into the basement in a cloud of dust. The next morning, the damage was discovered by workers who had arrived to install machinery and office furniture. The mess was sorted out, the floor rebuilt, and work resumed at the new location.

Meanwhile, McKnight had implemented his ideas to resolve the quality control problems that had plagued the business. In 1911, his fourth year with the company, he was brought back to St. Paul from Chicago. His approach to produce improvements was simple: ask the people who used the sandpaper in their factories for the answers. McKnight's sales practice involved getting the salesmen past the purchasing agent in the front office in order to show the product directly to the people who used it.

McKnight was persistent. He personally called on as many furniture plants as he could manage in a day. He wanted to know about the use of the products, including problems and complaints. He believed that the sales would grow through providing quality products rather than providing sales discounts. McKnight's approach to quality proved to be a turning point for Minnesota Mining and Manufacturing.

While McKnight was focused on products and customer service, Archie Bush was transferred to the Boston branch as office manager, perform-

Prior to mechanization such as this, abrasives were applied to sandpaper by hand.

ing bookkeeping, correspondence, and shipping duties. When a Boston salesman resigned, McKnight added sales to Bush's responsibilities. Bush was soon calling on the company clients including woodworking and shoe plants. 3M products were not yet reliable, and Bush had to replace products until the customer was satisfied.

Bush seemed to thrive in sales but even a great salesman can go through a slump. In 1914, Bush had a discouraging two-week lack of orders. When he received a letter from McKnight, Bush wondered if he was about to be fired. Instead, McKnight was sharing good news: McKnight had been appointed general manager and was now offering Bush the position of sales manager. The offer included an office in Chicago. Bush accepted the new job with pleasure. He completed his Boston work in three days and took the train to Chicago. He was twenty-seven years old.

Bush went after the highly competitive work in sales with imagination, energy, and commitment to efficiency. He made innovations in samples. He built new relationships with distribution houses. He trained their sales force about 3M products and paired them with 3M sales people. The sales force grew in numbers. Archie's life took shape around his work.

Archie's siblings were also establishing their adult lives and activities. Reuben married Hilda Haugen in 1916 and began a family, living near Granite Falls. Margaret was teaching school. After her additional education in a conservatory, Minnie signed up to work for the Red Cross in France following World War I, from 1918 to 1920. And the siblings' parents, Tom and Emma, moved off the farm and into Granite Falls in 1913.

In 1919, Archie Bush made a decision about his own personal life. He had progressed from $11.55 a week at a struggling start-up to a management position in a growing company and was earning $200 a month. After ten years with 3M he was ready to start his own home, buy a car, and settle in one place for a time. He had found the woman for him, actor and dancer Edith Bassler, a Chicago native. They married on November 8, 1919, and Edith (later spelled Edyth) turned her attention from her stage career to a role as wife of a busy Chicago executive.

6

Labs, Patents, and Growth at 3M

After the failure of corundum as an abrasive, the company switched to using Spanish garnet. When heavy seas resulted in a shipment of garnet being accidentally coated with a shipment of olive oil, the oily garnet would not adhere to the sandpaper. Two hundred tons of garnet had to be washed and heated in order to be used.

Following this hard and expensive lesson, the company processed any abrasive elements before application to the final product. By 1916, the company was testing materials not only at the outset of production, but through every stage of processing. Product testing and development were now the routine. Quality rose and customer complaints fell. New products were invented and others improved.

By the time World War I erupted in Europe, 3M had developed Three-M-ite, an aluminum oxide on cloth that was a durable, fast-working abrasive. This new product met Henry Ford's need for precision and speed in the polishing stages of car manufacture. In the first half of 1914 the gross sales of the product was $15,110. Over the next several years, the sales of Three-M-ite increased until it was 45% of total company sales.

The business was growing. More than a dozen automobile manufacturers were eager to use 3M abrasive products. By 1916, fourteen years after its founding, 3M had sixty-five employees, was free of debt, and declared a dividend of six cents a share.

By 1917, with the added demands for war goods, industry was absorbing all of 3M's capacity for product manufacture. Capital reserves enabled 3M to add to its St. Paul plant; a more spacious laboratory was created to meet the needs for new products and for product improvement. The company's line of abrasives became best-sellers and gross sales more than doubled in a short time. Board members began to receive pay for their services and were permitted to buy stock at a dollar per share. Stock prices rose to three dollars a share. By 1919, total company sales were $1,386,383 with a net profit of $439,407.

In the Chicago sales headquarters, run by Bush, the strong emphasis on client contact was maintained. Although salaries for salesmen were low, commissions were offered. 3M was expanding and executives like Bush were included in profit-sharing.

In 1921, Bush was promoted again, becoming a director and treasurer of the company. Four years later McKnight moved Bush to St. Paul to be general manager in charge of all sales. The sales force had grown to forty-eight: forty regulars, five commission men, and three foreign salesmen. Bush set a high standard for his staff and worked hard himself. He instituted regular sales meetings, worked on campaign approaches, and set quotas.

The company's creative new products brought them into the world of patent acquisition and purchase. One of its most successful creative new products, for which 3M became famous, was "Scotch tape."This innovative product emerged when the company acquired the patent for a self-sticking, waterproof tape. The tape had endless possibilities for use in industry, home and entertainment.

A new dustless abrasive, "WETORDRY" hit the market like a meteor and sales quadrupled. Its inventor, Francis G. Okie, joined the company as a laboratory employee and continued to find new applications for the dustless abrasive. The new products had the added benefit of reducing dangerous factory dust which caused illness and shortened lives. Initially, sales were slow due to the reluctance of old furniture factory hands to change from pumice to abrasive paper. The reluctance disappeared when the product's advantages were made obvious.

After thirteen years, a persistent sales effort by 3M brought WETORDRY to general acceptance. Due mostly to the automotive industry, the 3M product finally replaced less efficient methods of preparing metal surfaces. By now, not only new car makers but auto body repair shops became a substantial market for 3M's innovation. Sales climbed fast.

During the 1920's, 3M negotiated for foreign markets and set up plants in England, Germany, and France. In 1929 William L. McKnight was made president of the company.

Another major business breakthrough came in the 1930's when 3M entered into the weatherproof roofing business. A Wausau, Wisconsin, competitor was coating asphalt shingles with quartz in red, green, and yellow hues. It owned "a mountain of quartz" nearby. 3M bought out the competitor and launched a highly profitable and unique division.

The quartz granules reflected light and could be applied to paper-highlighted signs for road use. Sales zoomed again with "COLORQUARTZ." Between 1931 and 1935, A. G. Bush personally called on the roofing manufacturers, bringing along personnel for the new division. From these calls on more than twenty companies and an expansion of the division, sales volume grew spectacularly from $26,413 in 1932 to $255,379 in 1933 and $657,402 in 1934.

3M was working on many other product ideas, including one called masking tape. Dozens of ideas were being explored in the lab.

In spite of the economic downturn of the Great Depression, during the 1930's 3M grew and acquired additional plants, products, and functions. In 1932, sales were $3.4 million; in 1933, $4.7 million; in 1934, $5.9 million. Ten years later they totaled $62.9 million and in 1948, the last full years that Bush was directly responsible for sales, they reached $108.2 million.

Before World War I the annual sales had totaled $263,000. In thirty years, Minnesota Mining and Manufacturing had grown into a giant, adaptive company with world-wide sales.

7

This Man Bush

In 1925, Archie and his wife, Edyth, moved to St. Paul, Minnesota, where they built a home at 2215 Summit Avenue. The house, valued at $60,000, had six bedrooms, three baths, and a carriage house for staff. Living with them were Edyth's mother, her aunt, and the employees. The William McKnight family lived nearby.

The Bushes had no children but Archie's brother Reuben and his wife, Hilda, had two daughters, the only close relatives in that generation. The nieces had a cordial relationship with their uncle and remembered him with fondness for his generosity and good humor.

One of Archie's nieces, who attended St. Olaf College in Northfield, Minnesota, was a frequent guest at the Summit Avenue House. She described it as "a large two-story timbered house and it had a beautiful setting with large, tall trees, flower beds and shrubbery."

The front door led to a long drawing room where the visitor would see a fireplace, a large

Steinway piano, paintings, and a number of striking photographs of Aunt Edyth on the wall. The niece remebered being impressed by the down-filled sofa cushions on many davenports and chairs. Her uncle had an office or study close to the drawing room, "and there were many, many books in sets. He had a huge desk and chair."

Two smaller rooms were located off the drawing room—one a porch filled with plants, the other a similar screened retreat (no air conditioning in those days).

"One of the things I remember about the house," the niece continued, "was a beautiful, curved stairway from the foyer to the second floor, with a large tapestry hanging on the curved wall. I remember a beautiful crystal lamp on a marble-topped table in the foyer. It was always lighted as dusk fell, as a kind of welcome to my uncle Archie, especially in the fall and winter months."

Archie's niece remembered that the second floor had a master suite and three bedrooms and three baths besides. "My Aunt Edyth's mother and her Aunt Vic lived with them for many years, until they died. [Sarah Bassler died in 1938. Her husband Clarence had died in1906.] They were charming, tiny little ladies with white curly hair and we always enjoyed them."

Mrs. Bush had a French personal maid who chattered with her employer in French. Archie's niece noted that he was not particularly happy when the two conversed in French in his presence.

All of the staff lived in quarters above the two-car garage. The niece remembered a chauffeur, a cook, and a maid. "Those women wore uniforms, either gray or soft tan, with little white caps and white aprons. The chauffeur was dressed very plainly; he wore a business suit and shirt and tie and a visored cap. He also was charged with the upkeep of the yard." Going to his St. Paul office every day, Bush did paperwork as the chauffeur drove.

Bush's typical day started at 7 am, with him in the executive office before 9. His workday usually lasted until 5:30 p.m. His office was located at 900 Bush Avenue in St. Paul. Bush Avenue is a four-mile-long east-west street, which leads from central St. Paul through the 3M complex. The street, formerly Fauquier Street, was renamed Bush Avenue in 1957 in recognition of Archie Bush's "consistent, meritorious, pre-eminent and successful career in national and international fields and in cultural activities." Archie Bush was proclaimed "one of St. Paul's most respected citizens."

Archie drove his own automobile on trips out of St. Paul. He preferred Packards. Archie could conveniently visit his immediate family and large extended family in a day. When Archie drove out to Granite Falls to visit his brother Reuben, the two took long drives in the country. Archie's father and step-sister Sadie also had their home in nearby Granite Falls as did many of his aunts, uncles, and cousins.

Bush was described in the *3M Megaphone* as a "fastidious dresser, in a predominance of browns, tans and beige ... He is a cigar smoker, three or four a day, no cigarettes ... Evenings for the Bushes might include TV viewing, reading, a two-handed game of gin rummy, or bridge with friends. They attend St. Paul Civic Opera productions, musical concerts and other similar cultural events."

Edyth Bush resumed activity in the theater. Mr. Bush's niece recalled: "One time when I was a student at St. Olaf, Uncle Archie sent his car and the chauffeur there to bring me and my roommate to the Cities to see a show. I believe it was the play *La Gamine* at the Women's Club Assembly."

The *St. Paul Dispatch* announced the premiere: "Romance, rich color and highlights of dramatic intrigue will prevail at the premier of *La Gamine*, the play from the pen of Mrs. Archibald Bush of St. Paul. A group of well-known actors will present the play. The plot is said to lend itself admirably to the stage and screen. It concerns the romance of Charlotta Le Convrier, a French dancer, and the Archduke Ferdinand of Austria Hungary. For the play Mrs. Bush will wear a number of authentic gowns of the period of 1825 and 1827."

In 1939 Archie built and gave Edyth a theatre building near the intersection of Cleveland Avenue and Ford Parkway in St. Paul. She turned sixty that year and they had been married for twenty years. The Edyth Bush Little Theatre began productions in 1940. One of the missions of the theatre was to help local actors gain stage experience with working professionals. It was said that Archie made a practice of attending every play twice, once when the play opened and again for the last performance. He wished to see "if the actors had improved."

Mr. Bush heartily supported his wife's theater work. In the ground level of their Summit Avenue home was a very long room featuring a stage, complete with curtains. His niece recollected: "Behind the curtains was a lovely mural of a garden scene that had been the background in one of Aunt Edyth's plays, I think it was *La Gamine*.

"This recreation room downstairs was really lovely. All the rooms were lovely but this one fascinated me the most because of the stage. There was a smaller Steinway down there that had been made especially for Aunt Edyth by a member of the Steinway family and given to her. The house was full of gifts to her. I remember clocks, fifteen of them in the guest room where I stayed one time."

On December 1, 1964, Mrs. Bush donated the theater bearing her name to Hamline University. According to the *St. Paul Pioneer Press*: "This has since been a center for the development of amateur actors, directors and technicians, many of whom have gone on to brilliant theatrical careers."

Archie's niece reminisced about her uncle: "We really liked Uncle Archie. As I grew up, he made an impression on me as a very genial, kind, considerate and fun person, very warm, down to earth and practical. He was very kind and devoted to his family, to my grandfather (Thomas Bush) his father, and certainly to his half-sister, my Aunt Sadie. In short, he was the kind of man who would be happy to care for his mother-in-law and Aunt Vic to the end of their days."

"I remember when he came home, he would take a shower, then sit in the living room reading newspapers and business publications. We enjoyed the banter between Uncle Archie and Aunt Edyth. They seemed to enjoy being together. They had fun conversations and made up games and so on."

"As a teen-ager and in college, I had several opportunities to observe Uncle Archie. As a businessman he was very serious, hard working, direct and very knowledgeable about business. He had a very high standard of performance, both for himself and others. The first thing he observed about anyone coming to apply for a job was the shoes ... were they clean, were they polished. Physically, he was immaculate. He showered every morning and when he came home from work at night. He had a rather shiny, scrubbed look. He dressed conservatively, and always appropriately. His golf knickers always impressed me as a kid. They were the first

I had ever seen. Naturally I didn't see many ever."

"I believe that Uncle Archie and Aunt Edyth were Baptists; her family was Baptist. I don't think they went to church very often, but I have reason to believe they were Christian people who knew and loved the Lord."

He gradually reduced the seven-day work-weeks that had been necessary when he was helping build the company, and began to enjoy other activities and some leisure time, though he never quit working and always sought new worlds to conquer.

8

The Later Years

As the years advanced, Archie Bush began to transfer his responsibilities to others in the company, relinquishing his hands-on manner of management to pursue other interests. Though he would not have considered full retirement, he made a major change by establishing a winter home in Winter Park, Florida, near Orlando, in 1951.

In Florida the habits of a lifetime persisted. The Bush penchant for organization and promotion soon evidenced itself in the foundation of the Winter Park Commercial Bank and the Winter Park Memorial Hospital. He was chairman of the board at the bank and contributed generously to the hospital.

Bush had not been in Florida long before he was invited to serve on boards of business concerns and public service organizations, as he had in Minnesota: First National Bank of Winter Park, Builders Mortgage Company of St. Petersburg and Winter Park, General Guaranty Insurance Company, Central National Bank of

Jacksonville, and Rollins College.

At his home in Winter Park Archie used the library as his office, complete with a large executive desk. He followed a daily routine of opening the mail and dictating replies. His office had several telephone lines so that he could keep up with his numerous calls and conferences. Files were neatly arranged on the desk and on the windowsill behind his chair. He actively conducted considerable 3M business every morning, then broke for visits with nearby Winter Park associates and fellow investors and his Florida agricultural interests.

Archie began raising orange trees and cattle in Florida, perhaps a reflection of his youth as a farmer. He went at the citrus business just as he and his associates at 3M had tackled the making of sandpaper: "Let's see how we can do it better." Instead of setting out fifty to seventy-five trees to the acre (he owned 1700 acres) he planted ninety with the guidance of an experienced grower, Charles Bradshaw. They met their goal of 110,000 trees and sold the product to the juice concentrate line of the citrus business.

With the help of Charles Bradshaw, Bush was raising three- to four-thousand cattle by 1958. He had a primary role in the purchase, feeding, and sale of the livestock. His father, who had spent many years raising livestock and farming, saw none of this, having died in January of 1951 at age ninety-three.

Archibald and Edyth Bush at their home in Winter Park.
[photo courtesy the Bush Foundation]

Even with his farming and civic commitments in Florida, Bush did not abandon his Minnesota affiliations. He continued his support and interest in the Minneapolis and St. Louis Railway, St. Paul Foundation distribution committee, Hamline University, William Barnes Incorporated, American National Bank of St. Paul, St. Paul City Planning Board, James J. Hill Library, and Junior Achievement. The Greater St. Paul Community Chest honored him for his work there. He had been president of the World War Two "War Chest," a member of the United Defense Fund, the Hoover Commission, and Red Cross campaigns in St. Paul.

St. Paul's Hamline University became one of Archie's favorite charities. "Money doesn't grow on trees, but we can get it from a Bush," was the theme of a challenge fund at Hamline University in the late 1950's. Archibald G. Bush, chairman of the executive committee of 3M, offered $17,000 to the alumni association of the school, if the alumni could raise a like amount. The alumni only partly succeeded, according to an article in the *St. Paul Dispatch*. Bush's match came to $15,000. The next year, typical of one of the state's most successful sales managers, he added the $2,000 shortage and made the new challenge grant $19,000.

Archie was awarded an honorary doctorate by Hamline in 1956 and served on its board of trustees from 1957 until his death. He donated at least $800,000 to the new student center in 1963 and a significant amount to new library. According to the book, *Hamline University, a History*, he made provision that after his death, the university would receive $1 million a year for ten years. In 1970, four years after his death, Hamline received $517,000 from Edyth Bush and $600,000 from the Bush Foundation.

With his long career at 3M making him one of Minnesota's richest men, Archie Bush explored ways to be actively involved in sharing his wealth. He was particularly interested in young people on their way up, and decided that his financial success could be turned to philanthropy with purpose.

In 1953 he established the Bush Foundation as a means of moving his private assets into public action and benefit.

The year 1959 marked Bush's fiftieth year with 3M. He was seventy-two years old   In September, he was honored at the company's annual service awards affair at the St. Paul Civic Auditorium. Several hundred 3M employees and spouses attended the celebration. They looked back on half a century of an extraordinary Minnesota firm which had risen from debt-ridden failure to success in the global market. Since 1946 Minnesota Mining and Manufacturing had been listed on the New York Stock Exchange. With customers located around the globe, the company had offices in Australia, Brazil, Canada, France, Germany, Mexico, and the United Kingdom.

At the fifty-year anniversary, Bush said, "Looking ahead for the next fifty years, I'd say that if 3M continues along the pattern already established, it offers just as great an opportunity today as fifty years ago."

Bush could take credit for part of this 3M success, along with his colleague, William L. McKnight. For many years, Bush had successfully led the sales efforts. Through his persuasive leadership and encouragement, Bush had inspired many corporate employees.

Bush became one of the owners of 3M through his stock purchases in his early career. By 1929 he stopped acquiring 3M stock and developed other assets, in order to avoid a major stock price upset at his death. By the 1950's Bush, along with his wife Edythe, had 3M stock valued at about $125 million. A drop in share price of one dollar could mean a loss of more than a million dollars. However, a loss to his personal finances did not worry Bush. He told a reporter, "I have a friend in Florida who tells me he'd be drinking all the time if he had my money—drinking to forget his losses, drinking to celebrate the gains. I do neither." The only thing that worried Bush about a drop in market prices would be if it indicated loss of confidence in the 3M company.

He described his own attitude about personal finance as one focused on saving rather than relying on credit. "I saved money from the time I started working at $50 a month. It's tremendously important for a young man to save money. Save and invest—then you're ready for opportunity when it comes. Borrowing to invest, however, is a form of saving." He pointed out that opportunity still existed to build such a fortune as his.

He cited three rules for financial success:

1) Try for college, even though you may first have to work awhile and save for your tuition.

2) Remember that whatever business you're in, accomplishment is based on hard work, not wishful thinking.

3) Recognize the importance of making money for your employer as well as yourself—

once you become known as a money-maker, you get promotions.

Although Bush did not go to college when he left home in 1908, he built a great career on the education he acquired at business school.

Regarding his work in sales, Bush had not been an order-taker. He knew his products and what they would do and he knew his customer operations and requirements. He believed sales personnel had to be self-reliant, adaptive to each selling situation and able to think and talk on their feet.

Bush remembered his first sales call on a wood-working company in Lowell, Massachusetts, from which he got a small order. He felt it might have been his greatest sale because it proved to him that he could sell. He believed that if the product was right for the customer and the salesman worked hard to show it, the chances of success were good.

9

The Hometown Legacy: Granite Falls

The community surrounding Granite Falls, where Archie was born and raised, was never far from his heart and mind.

His parents, Emma and Tom, lived in Granite Falls until their deaths in 1928 and 1951. His siblings, Reuben Bush and Sadie Richardson, both of whom he visited regularly, lived in Granite Falls, too. His Hamre relatives, who Archie visited frequently, had businesses in the Granite Falls.

Bush, with his business acumen, saw that rural Minnesota was changing quickly. Granite Falls would have opportunities if they played their cards right. The local school superintendent, Milton Lindback, agreed. Lindback had arrived in Granite Falls in 1954. Lindback believed that in order to provide gainful employment the city needed expanded education facilities and industries. The resulting increased employment would produce more home ownership, additional housing, and an increased tax base. Lindback also wanted higher education in his district.

Lindback developed an exciting entrepreneurial relationship with Archie Bush, over a twelve year period. Bush encouraged his efforts and backed him up with practical aid.

Lindback explained the process to Tom Cherveny of the *Granite Falls Advocate Tribune* in 1993. "The [Minnesota] state department of industry had called with important information. A firm was interested in moving its operation and wanted to look at possible sites in Granite Falls. Could the school provide a bus to bring a group around town? ... The tour did not go well...The firm never came to town. For many, it was the final blow. An earlier effort to raise funds to bring an industry had already flopped."

Lindback decided to go out of town for help. "I went to see if Mr. Bush would help us out," said Lindback."

Lindback realized that Bush was just too busy a person to come around and see what he could do for Granite Falls, so Lindback went to Bush, offering to do the work for Bush if Bush would fund it. "Lindback said his knees knocked all the way down the hall as he approached Bush's office. Not much happened at the first meeting but things developed."

"Lindback was working on an effort for Granite Falls to have a four-year state college located here. Bush agreed to help, offering $500,000 in scholarship funds if the state chose Granite Falls. The college instead went to Marshall and is today's Southwest State University. Next, Lindback and Bush tried for a community college but that effort also failed." Ever persistent, they went to work to bring a technical school to Granite Falls and they were successful in this effort, the school opening in 1965.

Lindback had explained to Bush what Granite Falls had to offer. Bush responded by telling Lindback to find a suitable location for a seventy-acre industrial park. Bush purchased the site, located on the west side of Granite Falls, south of highway 212, in 1958. It had taken five years of effort from Lindback and Bush to create this opportunity for industrial growth.

The city didn't wait for the arrival of industry to express its appreciation to Archie Bush. In gratitude and recognition of Archie's generosity and support, the city of Granite Falls staged a Welcome Home event for him on October 20, 1958.

Mayor Aage Buhl issued the proclamation:
WHEREAS, Mr. Archibald G. Bush, esteemed former resident of this community, has seen fit to donate some of his talents toward a brighter future for Granite Falls by providing and developing additional grounds to attract other industries, homes and others to this city.

And WHEREAS, at this time, we should re-dedicate ourselves to support such unselfish endeavors, by setting aside a day in recognition thereof.

THEREFORE, I, Aage Buhl, Mayor of the city of Granite Falls, do proclaim Monday, October 20, 1958 as Archie Bush Appreciation Day and urge all citizens of this community to observe this day as such.

FURTHERMORE, I invite all to attend a dedication ceremony to be held on the Bush property, located south of highway 212 and west of 9th Street at 11 o'clock a.m. on said date, October 20, 1958.

The city made a gala of the Bush homecoming. The Jaycees constructed a speakers' platform at the site of the coming industrial park. All stores in Granite Falls closed for two hours so employees could attend the event. Parents took children out of school. KSTP-TV sent its helicopter from St. Paul to cover the event. Other broadcasters and reporters filed stories.

A welcoming committee, including police cars, fire trucks, civic officials, the school band, and the American Legion drill team, met the Bushes four miles east of town, just four miles south of Archie's birthplace. The cavalcade moved to the industrial park site where thousands of people welcomed them. There, the mayor gave Archie the key to the city and homecoming queen Barbara Lundell pre-

Archie Bush visiting with childhood friend, Christopher N. Holien and Clara Holien, 1958

sented flowers to Edyth Bush, Sadie Richardson, and Hilda Bush (Reuben's widow). A new street named Bush Drive ran along the industrial park.

After several short speeches, Mr. Bush took the microphone to describe his fond memories of Granite Falls, which he had always considered his hometown. He mentioned the many assets Granite Falls had to attract industry, and in closing, expressed the hope that "Granite Falls would become the head office of a good substantial industry." He said his property would not be given away but that he would be happy to make it available to an industry which would be of benefit to Granite Falls.

"I can assure you," he stated, "that if we can find the right industry which will help to meet the needs of the community which is sound financially, and which will make great community citizens, the cost or price of this industry will not stand in the way of progress. If what I have attempted to do proves to be of any assistance to this community, I'll feel that I have been well repaid." He had already spent something like $50,000 to purchase and prepare the site, described as being rough as "goat pasture," rock-strewn, and uneven.

Mr. Bush cut the ribbon which was attached to a bulldozer and the speaker's platform. As the ribbon parted, Mr. Bush climbed up to ride the bulldozer driven by Raydon Johnson on its first pass across the grounds. As he dismounted from the bulldozer someone attempted to brush some dirt off Archie's trousers, at which Archie said, "That's my dirt, I believe I can take that along with me."

After Archie dismounted from the bulldozer he was surrounded by life-long friends and family. Among them was his boyhood neighbor and fellow muskrat trapper, Christopher N. Holien. They had a good visit.

Meanwhile, Mrs. Bush remarked that she had never ridden on a fire engine. She was soon aboard the city fire engine as it roared down the street. This moment was captured by the local newspaper, the *Granite Falls Tribune*.

Following the events at the industrial site, the Bushes enjoyed a reception at the nearby home of Dr. and Mrs. John Lundquist. Mrs. Bush remarked she thought "it was the happiest day of Archie's life."

In appreciation of Granite Falls' warm reception, Mr. Bush sent the following letter to the *Granite Falls Tribune* for publication:

Mrs. Bush and I have no possible means of saying thank you to each and every one of the good people of Granite Falls who did so much to make Monday, October 20 such a pleasantly memorable day for us. Rather than trust our faulty memories to recall the names of all who so richly deserve our thanks we think it better to mention no names and ask of you one more favor.

Would you please be so kind as to publish our heartfelt thanks to one and all. It was very apparent to us from the moment we joined the caravan until we left for St. Paul, that many people had devoted hundreds of hours of careful thought and work to every detail of the day's program. I have been to many affairs in the Cities, but I do not recall having attended one that was so well organized, so totally devoid of minor speeches and so well suited to the occasion.

I like to think that one reason everything seemed so perfect is that it is just the result of what happens when old friends get together again. Again, Mrs. Bush and I want to say, thanks to the people of Granite Falls for everything.

Two months later, Mr. and Mrs. Bush sent the Granite Falls High School band a generous gift, as evidence of their close connection with the town following the "homecoming." The band had need of several new larger instruments to be provided for the use of young musicians.

Archie wrote:

> *The instruments you see before you are a Christmas gift from me and Mrs. Bush to the Granite Falls High School Band. My only opportunity to hear you play was at the A. G. Bush Appreciation Day ceremony. I was certainly impressed and pleased with your performance. The only obligation I want you to feel for this gift is an obligation to yourselves to produce a quality of music comparable to your ability. If you do this, I will feel well repaid for my effort in helping the Granite Falls instrumental music program. Merry Christmas and Happy New Year to all of you.*

This was only one of several substantial gifts to the school system over the years, probably guided by Lindback: School bus garage, overhead projectors for all classrooms, film strip projectors, tape recorders, copying machines, industrial arts shop equipment valued at over $22,000, more than $20,000 in scholarship monies for advanced education for teachers, summer school scholarships for juniors plus other unnamed gifts. Because of the teacher scholarships Lindback improved his staff, their teaching results and the recruitment for the school system.

Archie Bush had lived up to his stated belief: "Wealth should be used for the benefit of humanity."

In addition, Mrs. Bush gave $50,000 in 3M stock for the hospital and senior manor after Archie's death. The technical school, which had become a reality, was given a grant of $250,000.

On November 17, 1959, announcement came that a hydraulic manufacturing firm would locate at the Bush Industrial Park, and it was to be known at Granite Falls Hydraulics, Inc., a division of Rodgers Hydraulics of Minneapolis. Soon after, Plews Oilers, a manufacturer of products for auto services, set up a plant.

The Plews Oilers plant came almost by mistake, according to the *Granite Falls Advocate-Tribune*'s story of September 16, 1993. The first contact was made by Milt Lindback with Bush's cooperation, in a most serendipitous manner: "Unlike the Rodgers case, no one knew that Plews Oilers in downtown Minneapolis had any thoughts of moving. At that time a person from the State Department of Industrial Development called Lindback with a tip. A firm, whose name he could not give, was interested in moving. All he could tell Lindback was the number of employees it had, the size building it needed, and that it manufactured products for the automotive after-market."

"Lindback went to Bush's St. Paul office. Bush offered his secretary's help to go through a registry of businesses. Lindback was looking for a needle in a haystack, hoping he could find a company that matched the description he had. He found the

wrong company. Plews Oilers matched the description, but it was not the company the state man had
given the tip about. Lindback and Bush did not
know that, and Bush agreed to call Plews Oilers.
The president was dumbfounded that Bush knew
they were looking to move. Only he and his banker
had ever discussed the possibility. Bush explained
the situation and it became a joke among the men."

The impact on the local job and economic
scene was impressive. In 1962 the *Granite Falls
Tribune* summarized: "The contributions of Mr.
Bush to Granite Falls in the way of gifts to the
schools and other institutions, his development of
the industrial site and establishment of an industrial center there are of the greatest importance to
the city. He has given us an example of what can
be done by the exercise of personal initiative and
sustained effort; he has given the city an opportunity to prove that in helping the city to help itself
he has given us not only hope for the future, but an
opportunity and an obligation to work for that future in the development of a city and its economy,
which will justify and bring to fruition Mr. Bush's
hopes for Granite Falls."

More important than the financial gifts Bush
made, (even though they were substantial) was
the attitude for economic development which
Bush and Lindback stimulated in the minds of
the community leaders. Many small towns were
losing population and businesses at a time when

they were also facing costly infrastructures repairs. The challenge for Granite Falls was to stimulate growth and attract industry.

The first two industries on the scene were Rogers Hydraulics and Plews Oilers. This was followed by the addition of a vocational-technical school which provided a source of training for the plants. All three of these entities were secured through Bush's encouragement and financial backing.

It was no accident that Bush invited Rodgers Hydraulics to occupy the first site at the Granite Falls Industrial Park. Fluid power appeared to be the workhorse of the future.

In contrast, Plews Oilers provided a different type of factory work involving metal fabrication.

The vocational technical school, which opened in 1965, was soon providing workers for Victor Fluid Power and Plews Oilers, as well as other local industries. The demand for trained workers required the enlargement of the vocation technical school campus. On-site training programs were added as well as creation of the Bush Student Center and Lindback Library. Several vocation school graduates started their own businesses. As a result of all these activities, local wage levels rose. Granite Falls and the surrounding areas experienced an improved quality of life. The vision shared by Bush and Lindback became reality.

From the *Granite Falls Advocate Tribune*, 1993: "The relationship between Lindback and Bush would change the shape of Granite Falls school district and the community itself." At this point in 1993, Lindback said, Bush had provided between $400,000 and $500,000 to this community. Much of it was earmarked for the school."

Over time, the vocational technical school offered classes in a wide range of subjects: fluid power, (the first in the nation with a two-year program), business, real estate, insurance, day care, accounting, food service, dietetic management, electrical and boiler operations, business management, safety, farm business management, appliance repair, welding, car care, photography and many community education interests.

The vocation technical school began as a post-secondary institution with two-year courses but eventually won college status as part of the degree program of the Minnesota Department of Education. Along with educational institutions in Canby, Jackson, Pipestone, and Worthington, it became part of the Minnesota West Community and Technical College system.

Along with wage improvements, other benefits also accrued from the industries and school. New people arrived and the population of Granite Falls grew from 1970 on. Unemployment figures were very low, lower than the national average. Personal income rose county-wide. Property values rose three-fold in twenty-five years, adding significantly to the tax base. Building permits for homes and commercial buildings rose steadily. Infrastructures were improved. The hospital and manor home were renovated. More workers and students were trained and new careers built. High quality products were manufactured and distributed all over the world. Because businesses and industries needed shipping capacity, UPS chose Granite Falls as its central operation point in the area.

The Bush Industrial Park was only the beginning. Now that the example had been set and the lesson of Bush enterprise learned, Granite Falls was busy attending to its business. The biggest project was the addition of a second industrial park on the east side of the city, over 200 acres of farmland annexed. Here several smaller industries took root and the first grass landing airstrip for business and recreational airplanes was laid out. Highway access improved with the routing of county roads along the new acreage.

Sunsource Fauver moved in and soon expanded with more operational space. On the horizon was MNVAP, a farmer-owned cooperative organized to process alfalfa as an alternative energy source for electricity. Ahead soon was the Fagen, Inc decision to build a $1.5 million headquarters for construction and engineering, which has since only increased in impact.

The process for construction of a fully modern airport was a lengthy one, but finally, in 1995, the plan was approved by the state, with no drain on annual tax rolls. (A hospital surplus was used for a loan within the city.) This airport approval was an important element tipping the Fagen, Inc. decision towards Granite Falls over the competitors. Fagen provided the evacuation of the old airfield from 1975 to the new airport, making more acres available for new industry.

Project Turnabout, a major employer providing private treatment for drug, alcohol, and gambling addictions, received a $200,00 grant from the Bush Foundation. In 1988, the organization left its first location in the old Tuberculosis Sanitorium for a large facility in the Northwest part of Granite Falls.

The Granite Falls Community, motivated by the generous example set by Bush, created and implemented a vision for the future. One achievement, thanks to a state partnership for community improvement, was the approval and construction of a multi-purpose community center, with meeting, athletic, and swimming facilities. Another improvement was the significant enlargement and re-design of the city library.

The city of Granite Falls entered a long-term planning program in 1998, under provisions of a 1998 state law. Three counties began public meetings in 1999, receiving citizen input in a region reaching from Granite Falls northwest to the source of the Minnesota River. The planning was for a pilot project involving land use, housing, and development.

In place of Archie Bush's direct participation, the Bush Foundation and other funding partners took on effective roles. Instead of Lindback, the city had an Economic Development Authority, concerned with industry, commercial, and housing. Working with this authority were the local banks as well as government agencies for the acquisition of grants, loans, and programs. The Southwest Minnesota Initiative Fund, a specific outgrowth of the McKnight Foundation in the 1980's, played a part.

The life of Archibald G. Bush can be measured in decades, years, months, and days, but his legacy is immeasurable, both through his own direct gifts and those of his foundation. The Granite Falls Public School, the tech school, the industries, the teachers, the students, the workers, the medical and business entities—all were deeply changed over time. Tens of thousands of individuals in the entire region benefitted from improvements that emerged through the city's industries and institutions.

Archie Bush was an uncommon "common man," respected for his success and loved for his thoughtful charity. He may not be recognized by a marble statue but he lives on through his thoughtful legacy to his hometown. Lessons he learned on the farm about personal responsibility within a shared working community propelled his generosity and purposes for his hometown.

His gifts continue to grow and impact the people of the area.

The entire personal circle back to Granite Falls had been made by Archie Bush. His hometown. His history, his family and their history:

Tom and Emma Bush had moved into the city of Granite Falls in 1913, when Tom was fifty-five and Emma sixty-four. Their two youngest children had finished high school. For decades they lived in a two-story home on Eighth Avenue, near downtown. The family became members of the Congregational Church, one of the churches in Granite Falls that used the English language consistently.

Emma Ingeborg Hamre Richardson Bush, nearly 79, died on September 15, 1928, after a long illness. She had borne eight children, raised five, and made decisions that directed their lives. Her obituary in the *Granite Falls Tribune* described her as "one of God's true handmaidens. She is said to have been a diligent worker in the Congregational Ladies Aid, as well as showing a keen interest in all the departments of the church. For years she was an active member and in recent years was made a life member of the Women's Christian Temperance Union. Her disposition won her a large circle of friends and her attention to all things of good, established within her that character which reached out and touched the hearts and souls of those around her and built her assurance of eternal life." She was buried in the Granite Falls City Cemetery.

Tom Bush served as city assessor for sixteen years, according to his obituary in the *Granite Falls*

Tribune for January 25, 1951. "He was a student of politics and took a keen interest in local government." He died on January 16, 1951, at age ninety-three and was buried in the Granite Falls City Cemetery.

Sadie Richardson moved to Granite Falls with her parents and lived there for the rest of her life. For at least twenty years she had a millinery and dressmaking business in town. According to the *Tribune*, she left that business in 1928, the year her mother died, and managed the household for her stepfather, Tom. She had many interests and was a founding member of the Tuesday Study Club and the League of Women Voters. Sadie died at age eighty-four on March 13, 1960, and after services at the Congregational Church, was buried in the Granite Falls City Cemetery next to her parents.

Reuben William, the eldest Bush son, remained in Granite Falls and was a farmer and businessman until his death at seventy-three on October 29, 1957. His home was located at the Asbury railroad crossing, five miles north of Granite Falls. At one time he operated a service station there. He held public office in Granite Falls and was secretary for the Granite Falls Kiwanis Club. Reuben married Hilda Haugen on June 17, 1916, and they had two daughters, Ione and Harriet. Reuben and Hilda belonged to the Granite Falls Lutheran Church and were buried in the Hillcrest Cemetery.

Archibald Granville Bush died on January 16, 1966, at Winter Park, Florida. His funeral was held at Hamline Methodist Church and burial in the Oakland Cemetery, St. Paul. He was seventy-eight. The fourteen 3M company directors were honorary pallbearers. The Bush Foundation, which he created in 1953, continues to this day, funding and guiding for the purposes Archie intended.

Margaret Louise Bush went to the East Granite Falls School three miles from the farm, as is confirmed by a 1901 picture at the school. She graduated from Granite Falls High School in 1909 and became a schoolteacher. In February of 1922, at Granite Falls, she married Aurel Hollensteiner, a Montanan. He died less than a month after the marriage, in March, possibly at the Mayo Clinic in Rochester, Minnesota. Margaret continued her teaching career and was working in the Missoula schools in 1955. She lived in St. Paul in her retirement years, where she died at age seventy-nine in October, 1968. She, too, was buried near her parents in the Granite Falls City Cemetery.

Minnie Grace, the youngest of the Bush children, also went to the East Granite Falls School and graduated from the high school in 1910. In 1918 she applied for a passport and sailed to France to work for the Red Cross during the First World War I. She returned, sailing from Antwerp to New York, two years later, in 1920. After a stay with her parents, she moved permanently to New

York, where she remained for nearly fifty years. She died on July 19, 1969, and was buried next to her family in the Granite Falls City Cemetery after services at the Congregational Church.

Archie's grandfather Amund, his wife Dorte, and five of their eight children, (Archie's uncles and aunt), were buried in Granite Falls City Cemetery. Archie's great uncle Helge and wife Else, who were Archie's godparents, were buried in Granite Falls Hillcrest Cemetery, later followed by their family members.

Edyth Bassler Bush, widow of Archibald G. Bush, followed him in death by six years, on November 20, 1972. She was ninety-three and had been living in Florida for the interim period. After her husband's death in 1966, Mrs. Bush established the Edyth Bush Charitable Foundation, Inc., of Orlando and Winter Park, Florida. The lawyer, H. Clifford Lee, who worked on the creation of her foundation and eventually chaired it, was originally from Granite Falls, and had been city attorney during the Bush activities of the 1950's. Lee's mother and father had been attorneys and judges in town. A large proportion of the Edyth Bush funds were disbursed to organizations based in central Florida. Edyth was buried in St. Paul, next to her husband.

10

The Bush Foundation

[contributed by foundation staff]

"Wealth should be used for the benefit of all humanity."

– Archibald G. Bush

The work of the Bush Foundation is a living legacy of Archie Bush. The Foundation is actively addressing the challenges of today in ways that are rooted in the life and the philanthropy of its founder. In total, the Foundation has given more than $1.5 billion to individuals and communities—an extraordinary extension of Archie's lifelong generosity.

EARLY HISTORY

The Bush Foundation was incorporated on February 24, 1953, "to encourage and promote charitable, scientific, literary and educational efforts." Archie was elected President of the Foundation at the first meeting and was actively engaged in Foundation business.

In the early days, much of the funding went to civic and human service organizations in St. Paul and to direct gifts to individuals experiencing hardship or seeking educational opportunity. As the years went on, the Foundation got more specific about priorities. In the two annual reports published while Archie was living (1963 and 1964), the Foundation described itself as "most active in the areas of college and schools; student aid; leadership development; prevention of and social problems related to alcoholism; and general welfare."

The Foundation also started taking on bigger and more ambitious projects over time. One of the most notable was Granville House (which carries the middle name of Archie and his father), a residential program for women with alcoholism located in St. Paul founded in 1963. The Foundation purchased the property, funded its startup costs, and collaborated closely with public and private partners to establish the residence and its programming.

One of the most significant programs established under Archie's leadership was the Bush Fellows program—still a flagship program for the Foundation. It was launched in 1964 for Minnesota men between the ages of 25 and 40. It was a two-year self-designed program, supporting one year of academic study and one year serving as an assistant to an outstanding leader in business, government, education or a union. People who knew Archie described it as the type of program he wished had been available to him as a young man. As with all the Foundation's programs, the Fellowship has evolved and changed over time—for example, it was expanded to include women in 1972.

When Archie died in 1966, he left the bulk of his estate to the Bush Foundation with Edyth's written consent. Within months of Archie's death, a ten-year struggle began over control of the Foundation, finally resolving in 1976.[1] During this difficult decade of board infighting, the Foundation

---

1. Some board members wanted to move the Foundation and its assets to Florida, where Edyth lived. Toward that end, Edyth announced her intention to renounce the will. The Minnesota Governor's office got involved in negotiating a financial compromise approved in August of 1966 by the Ramsey County Probate Court for Edyth to release her claims on the estate. That agreement did not end the legal challenges. There were numerous lawsuits and countersuits brought by board directors. The Minnesota Attorney General was directly engaged with the Foundation as these lawsuits played out over the decade in both Minnesota and Florida courts. The legal challenges continued after Edyth suffered a debilitating stroke in 1968 and was ruled incompetent, and after her death in 1972. It was not until 1976 that the Ramsey County Probate Court released the second half of Archie's estate that they had been holding until the legal disputes were settled. In 1978, the board amended the governing documents to remove any family member designation and the Foundation has had independent board governance since that time. The Edyth Bush Charitable Foundation was established in 1966 and is based in Winter Park, Florida. In recent years, the two Foundations have collaborated on grantmaking to honor Archie and Edyth.

added professional staff and began grantmaking on a larger scale through more formalized processes.

GRANTMAKING

While Archie was alive, Foundation giving was primarily focused on St. Paul with occasional gifts to Chicago (like the gift to establish the A.G. Bush Library of Management, Organization and Industrial Relations at the University of Chicago in 1959) and other places where the Bush family had ties. After Archie died and the Foundation's size was dramatically increased by the assets from his estate, the board expanded its geographic focus. Through the years, this has included some significant national grantmaking (like a thirty-year program with Hewlett Foundation that invested $52 million in Historically Black Colleges and Universities, starting in 1976). Today the focus of grantmaking is Minnesota, North Dakota, South Dakota and the twenty-three Native nations that share that geography.

The Foundation's tagline, and its strategy, is to "invest in great ideas and the people who power them." This reflects its roots in 3M innovation and in Archie's people-focused approach to philanthropy.

INVESTING IN IDEAS

Through the years, the Foundation has helped develop, test and spread great ideas around the region and across the country. For example, the Foundation:

– funded the creation of the first domestic violence shelter in the U.S. in 1974, as well as funding an innovative community domestic abuse response approach, known as the "Duluth model," that has spread nationally.

– was an early funder in early childhood development, which included creating Bush Centers for child development and social policy at University of Michigan, University of North Carolina, UCLA and Yale. Their work helped establish the field in the late 1970s and 1980s.

– has promoted the idea of nation-building, supporting tribes to build governance capacity and exercise sovereignty to solve their people's challenges. This work grew from grants like those in the 1990s to build tribal law libraries and tribal court capacity, and developed into a full strategic initiative including the creation of the Native Nation Rebuilders program and the Native Governance Center.

The work of developing, testing and spreading ideas continues today. Recent grants include investing in the first tribally owned power authority, funding new approaches to agricultural finance, and supporting the first accredited law school program for incarcerated people. And the ongoing impact of past grantmaking is visible all across the region including in the major gifts given through the years to build up colleges and arts organizations.

INVESTING IN PEOPLE

The Foundation continues to invest directly in people.[2] The Bush Fellowship program has changed through the years, including dedicated programs in the past for the arts and medicine. Altogether, the Foundation has selected nearly 2,500 Bush Fellows, investing roughly $100 million in their growth. Bush Fellows through the years have included people such as:

– August Wilson, who used his fellowship to write the play "Fences," which went on to win Tony Awards and the Pulitzer Prize for drama.

– Alyce Spotted Bear, a chairwoman of the MHA Nation who became a leading national voice on issues of Native education and youth.

– Michael Osterholm, PhD, MPH, an epidemiologist who has been a leading national and global advisor throughout the COVID-19 pandemic.

– Sean Sherman, aka the "Sioux Chef," a James Beard-winning chef who is a leader in the Indig-

---

2. Funding individuals is unusual in private foundations and is largely prohibited in the 1969 Tax Reform Act. The Bush Foundation received special permission from the IRS to continue its Bush Fellows program and continues to operate today within the bounds of that permission.

enous food movement in the region and around the world.

– Andrea Jenkins, a poet who went on to become president of the Minneapolis City Council and the first African American trans woman to win elected office in the U.S.

– Kevin Killer, a former South Dakota state-elected official who is now serving as president of the Oglala Sioux Tribe.

The Foundation's commitment to leadership extends beyond the Bush Fellowship program. The Foundation funds other programs that invest in individuals as well as leadership networks that inspire, equip and connect people to lead more effectively. For example, the Foundation funded the startup of the Josie R. Johnson Leadership Academy, operated by the African American Leadership Forum, and provided the first grant funding for the Coalition of Asian American Leaders.

MAKING THE REGION BETTER FOR EVERYONE

The Foundation's purpose statement is "to inspire and support creative problem solving—within and across sectors—to make the region better for everyone." This reflects a focus on the capacity of the people in the region to address any and all challenges that come their way. And it reflects the Foundation's deep commitment to equity, with particular focus on rural communities and racial justice.

This commitment has roots in Archie's life and leadership. At the very first Foundation board meeting in 1953, Archie and his fellow board members approved a resolution to be inclusive of all people, regardless of race or national origin. This commitment was evident across the Foundation's work. For example, the first-ever class of Bush Fellows in 1965 was racially diverse and included the leader of the state's task force on racial equality.

In 2020, the Foundation issued $100 million in social impact bonds to create two community trust funds to support Black and Indigenous individuals to go to school, buy a house, start a business or other wealth-building activities. This was a reparative act to address racial wealth gaps that have built up over many decades and reflect the accumulated impact of race-based discrimination throughout our country's history. It is also a strategy—supporting individual initiative and development—that is a very Archie way of doing philanthropy.

When he established the Foundation, Archie gave its future staff and directors enormous flexibility. This allows the Foundation to be creative and adaptable while still honoring Archie's donor intent. As is written into the Foundation's operating values, staff and board *never lose sight of the reason we exist: to do the most possible good with the resources left to the community by Archibald G. Bush.*

Epilogue

– David Smiglewski

Bush Fellow and
Granite Falls Mayor

The lasting legacy of Archie Bush in his home-town speaks not only of his generosity but also his vision and his commitment to investing in education, in people, their ideas and their future. That support has lent itself to entrepreneurs of all stripes, as well as those who aspire to be.

You have read about Archie Bush's remarkable life and success. You have also read about his philan-thropy and how it supported his hometown's need for new employment opportunities and how that generosity has inspired Granite Falls to reach for and achieve a new and more self-sustaining future.

But perhaps the most important aspect of Ar-chie Bush's continuing legacy in Granite Falls is the realization that good and productive things can indeed happen here, that value-added agriculture and manufacturing can take seed and grow and prosper here, and that empowering people's educa-tion and spirit is foundational to the financing of, and investing in, new ideas and new ventures.

That legacy continues today and underscores the ongoing evolution of the Granite Falls community and the local economy. New and evolving developments include a wholesale diversifying of the local economy which includes both new businesses in new buildings and repurposing existing buildings for new uses, by new or expanding businesses.

The former Rogers Hydraulics/Victor Fluid Power (VFP) building was, in 2002, occupied by Specialty Systems, Inc., a manufacturer of a variety of large industrial equipment, primarily for railroad maintenance use but also other custom-built industrial and construction-related products that are shipped world-wide.

The former Rogers Hydraulics line of presses, pumps and jacks was purchased by five former Rogers/VFP employees who started a new business known as Granite Fluid Power. They set up shop in the building that had once been the school district's large bus garage. Built in the 1960s, with a donation to the school district by Archie Bush to free up existing space for industrial trades classes in the school, the bus garage had been leased by private school bus operator Bennett and Bennett, a local concern that took over school bus operations several years ago. The bus garage building had been damaged in the July 25, 2000, tornado that struck the west end of Granite Falls and was sold to a private individual who repaired it and then sold it to the new

Granite Fluid Power enterprise. Bennett and Bennett constructed a larger bus facility in the city's expanded industrial park in the Highland Park Addition on the Chippewa County side of Granite Falls.

Also sustaining severe damage in the 2000 tornado were three buildings at the growing Project Turnabout treatment center campus, including two buildings that were less than a year old, and to which the Bush Foundation had made a major financial donation. While reconstruction of the campus was underway following the tornado, Project Turnabout temporarily occupied vacant space at the former state hospital site in Willmar. They kept all employees on board and committed to build bigger and better in Granite Falls. That effort resulted in a totally new campus that was better suited for up-to-date treatment needs and was expanded in 2013 with a new and larger wing for women and an additional wing for men. The treatment center was expanded again in 2019 and now has room for 131 patients in their residential chemical dependency and gambling addiction treatment programs in Granite Falls.

Project Turnabout also offers outpatient treatment programs in Granite Falls as well as Willmar, Redwood Falls and Marshall, where they also have a twenty-four-bed halfway house for men. They also have sober houses for men and for women in Willmar and are constructing a sixteen-bed halfway house for women in Willmar that will also feature an innovative program for job training in collaboration with Ridgewater College. That is expected to open in late 2021. The Bush Foundation has been a supporter and a benefactor to Project Turnabout with generous donations for other capital needs, as well as programming needs.

The 200,000 square foot building once occupied by Plews/Parker Hannifin was purchased by Fagen Inc. a number of years ago and converted to their construction equipment and supply depot and construction equipment shop. They also set up an area for manufacturing and fabricating construction related equipment which was recently expanded for overhead lifting capabilities.

Among other new industrial operations in Granite Falls are the former Marr Valve, now known as The Specialty Manufacturing Co., which, after outgrowing their building in downtown Granite, constructed a new manufacturing facility in the Highland Park Industrial Park next to the expanded Minnesota Feed Distributors warehouse. They manufacture components for use in dental equipment and equipment for other medical-related uses.

The building they had once occupied in downtown Granite is now owned by the Granite Falls Economic Development Authority and is occupied by a new firm, Granite Falls Woodworks, which is engaged in making custom wood counter-tops and other custom wood products. The firm is owned and operated by three local former employees of a wood cabinet manufacturer formerly located in nearby Wood Lake.

Par Piping has been located in the Highland Park Industrial Park for over twenty years and has recently expanded their manufacturing facilities. They fabricate a wide variety of stainless-steel products used in agriculture commodity processing and dairy processing.

In 2018, Van Diest Supply Company expanded their reach into Minnesota by building a large distribution warehouse in the Highland Park Industrial Park for wholesale supplying of agriculture and farm chemicals to their retail customers in a large part of southwestern and west-central Minnesota.

Nearby, E and H Piping, LLC, in 2020 built a large equipment shop for their ag processing and grain handling construction business.

The largest industrial facility in Granite Falls was built by Granite Falls Community Ethanol, now known as Granite Falls Energy, LLC (GFE). Their $60 million, fifty million gallons per year capacity facility was constructed on land that was annexed into the east portion of the city in 2006. The initial impetus for the establishment of GFE was replacing the Farmer's Cooperative Elevator grain elevator and grain handing facilities which were destroyed in the July 2000 tornado. Instead of rebuilding on their small footprint of land on the west end of Granite, the elevator company along with Fagen, Inc., helped organize a new enterprise that led to the building of the corn to ethanol facility at the junction of Highways 212 and 23, east of the city. After launching, the facility has grown and now boasts 40 employees and generates additional income for area farmers and shareholders in the firm. As GFE has grown, the company has taken a majority ownership position in the similar-sized Heron Lake BioEnergy ethanol plant in that Minnesota city.

A bright star was added to the Granite Falls community when Pioneer PBS decided to accept the gift of a new broadcast center from the Ron and Diane Fagen Family Foundation. The nearly $7 million donation was announced in late 2015 with construction commencing in 2016. Upon completion in 2017, Pioneer PBS moved their operations from Appleton to the new studio located along Highway 23 on the south edge of Granite Falls. The generosity of the Fagen Family made this possible and that donation has resulted in several employees moving to Granite Falls as well as a steady stream of employees and guests coming here for program appearances.

And some new and perhaps somewhat overdue aspects to the local economy in Granite Falls that has taken root here is tourism and the arts. While the scenic beauty of the Minnesota

River Valley and the cultural history of the area has always been an attraction, there is an impressive list of several new developments in recent years that have added to the list of reasons to visit the area.

Prairie's Edge Casino Resort, owned and operated by the Upper Sioux Community and located just three miles south of Granite Falls features a large gaming area as well as a spacious convention and entertainment center and a hotel with 160 rooms and suites as well as a RV campground with 42 sites close to the casino resort. As you might guess Prairie's Edge is one of Yellow Medicine County's largest employers.

Nearby, at the newly expanded Granite Falls Municipal Airport is the amazing Fagen Fighter's World War II Museum that features Ron Fagen's extensive collection of carefully restored and fully operational World War II airplanes and fighting aircraft as well as other World War II vehicles and displays, including a display about the Nazi-led Holocaust genocide of European Jews. The Fagen Fighters World War II Museum has received wide attention and hosted visitors from across the United States and several foreign countries.

Adding to the tourism economy of Granite Falls is a new and growing art scene with the KK Berge Gallery and the YES House performance space in downtown Granite Falls as well as several new displays of public art that have captured the imagination of residents and visitors along the scenic riverside downtown area.

And the Minnesota West Community and Technical College campus, which Archie Bush helped finance (and which has a building named after him) has continued to evolve with the times, adding general studies classes that can be applied toward a four-year degree as well as new and revised trade programs. The campus also has intensive computer-related programs and has added a nursing program as well as an electrical line technician program and will soon offer an expanded welding program.

Archie Bush was generous to the municipal hospital in Granite Falls and the hospital has forged ahead with health care improvements recently, completing a new nursing home in 2014, near the site of the hospital's congregate residential facility in the Highland Park area of the community. After affiliating with Avera Healthcare System, the local hospital leadership team is making plans to build a new hospital facility near the nursing home, establishing what will be a health-care campus.

Nothing ever remains static. Communities must adapt and keep pace with changing conditions, including a response to ever-evolving economics. However, the capability and work ethic of the people in that community are virtues not to be denied. Archie Bush's belief and the Bush

Foundation's continuing work in support of those virtues and the financial support they have historically offered has proven to be a continuing factor in his hometown of Granite Falls

That legacy of generosity has continued with the Bush Foundation's gift of $100,000 to the Yellow Medicine East School District in 2013, which marked the Foundation's 60th anniversary. The gift was used to construct a state-of-the-art, controlled environment greenhouse for science and agriculture classes.

That Bush Foundation's legacy of fondness for Archie Bush's hometown continues today with a recent $200,000 grant to be used for a purpose of the community's choosing, a $1 million endowment grant to the Granite Falls Area Community Foundation and the establishment of the Archie Bush Legacy Scholarship program which funds scholarships and support and support for students graduating from Yellow Medicine East High School to attend two-year and four-year colleges.

Archie Bush's legacy and generosity have certainly made an indelible mark on the Granite Falls area and has inspired a confidence in residents that the future is their hands and will indeed be bright.

Timeline

1848 Ingeborg Amundsdatter Hamre born in Norway to Amund Helgeson Hamre and Marit Knutsdatter Fygle.

1858 Thomas Granville Bush born in West Virginia to Isaac and Louisa Miner Bush.

1866 Ingeborg Hamre emigrates to America. Thomas Granville Bush moves with his family to Texas.

1871 Ingeborg Hamre's cousins, the Holien-Fygle family, come to America.

1875 Ingeborg Hamre marries William Richardson.

1876 Ingeborg (Hamre) and William Richardson's first child, Sadie Ann Richardson is born. Three later children do not survive past 1883.

1879 Birth of Edith Bassler in Chicago, Illinois. Ingeborg Hamre's brother, Helge, emigrates to Minnesota.

1880 Death of Ingeborg's husband, William Richardson.

1881 Ingeborg (Hamre) Richardson's father, Amund, emigrates to Minnesota.

1882 Ingeborg/Emma Richardson buys Minnesota farmland. Her step-mother and half-siblings join Amund Hamre in Minnesota.

1883 Ingeborg/Emma Richardson marries Thomas Granville Bush in Oklahoma and they move to Texas.

1884   Reuben William Bush is born in Texas.

1885   The Bush family moves to Wang Township, Renville County, Minnesota. Ingeborg/Emma buys more farmland. She is reunited with her father and his family who farm right next to Emma and Thomas Bush.

1887   Birth of Archibald Granville Bush, March 5.

1889   Birth of Margaret Louise Bush.

1890   Archibald, Reuben and Margaret Bush are baptized in the Norwegian Lutheran faith, Wang Church.

1892   Birth of Minnie Grace Bush.

1895   Bush Family lives in Wang Township for the first 5 months of the year, then moves to a rented farm close to Granite Falls. Minnie Grace Bush is baptized at Vestre Sogn Church.

1901   Amund Hamre buys and moves to a farm in the adjoining township of Hawk Creek.

1902   In Two Harbors, Minnesota, a small mining company (later 3M) gets started.

1903   The Thomas and Emma Bush family returns to her farm in Wang Township and lives in a large, newly-built farmhouse.

1905   In Two Harbors, Minnesota, an investor named Ordway bolsters the struggling young sandpaper company.

1907   In Two Harbors, Minnesota, a farm boy from South Dakota, William McKnight is hired as assistant bookkeeper by Minnesota Mining and Manufacturing.

1908   Archie Bush leaves home and moves to the Lake

Superior area, working building docks to earn enough
money to go to business school for four months in
Duluth.

1909   In April, Archie Bush is hired by Minnesota
Mining and Manufacturing to take over McKnight's
job as assistant bookkeeper, earning $11.55 a week.

1910   The federal census lists Archie Bush under the
Tom Bush household, citing that he is working in the
office of a manufacturing company.

Minnesota Mining and Manufacturing moves its
operation to St. Paul. Archie Bush is sent to take over
the branch office in Boston.

1912   Archie Bush adds sales to his Boston
responsibilities.

1914   Archie Bush is promoted and is transferred
to the Chicago office. Minnesota Mining and
Manufacturing produces its first abrasive cloth.

1916   Archie's brother, Reuben Bush, marries Hilda
Haugen in Granite Falls, Minnesota.

Minnesota Mining and Manufacturing produces Thee-
M-ite and builds a lab.

1918   Archie's sister, Minnie Bush, goes to World
War I France, working for the Red Cross.

1919   Archie Bush and Edith Bassler are married in
Chicago, Illinois on November 8.

1920   Minnie Bush returns from France, sailing from
Antwerp, Belgium to New York, and visits her parents
in Granite Falls before moving to New York.

1921 Archie Bush is promoted to treasurer and director of the Minnesota Mining and Manufacturing company.

1922 Archie's sister, Margaret Bush marries Aurel Hollensteiner in Granite Falls in February. He dies less than a month later, on March 4, probably at the Mayo Clinic in Rochester, Minnesota.

1923 Grandfather Amund Hamre dies and is buried Granite Falls City Cemetery.

1925 Archie and Edith (now spelled Edythe) move to St. Paul, Minnesota, and he is named general manager of all company sales.

1926 Archie and Edythe move into a new six-bedroom home at 2215 Summit Avenue, St. Paul. Her mother and aunt live with them until their deaths.

Minnesota Mining and Manufacturing is making masking tape and a new cellophane tape.

1928 Ingeborg/Emma Bush dies and is buried in Granite Falls City Cemetery. Sadie Richardson retires from her millinery business and takes up the housekeeping for her stepfather, Tom Bush.

1930 Federal census reports the Bush home on Summit Avenue is valued at $60,000. He is the vice president of a sandpaper factory and has a radio set. Living with them is Edythe's mother, Sarah/Sadie Bassler and her aunt, Victoria Nason, and Emma Quost, probably staff.

1937 Minnesota Mining and Manufacturing builds new labs for innovation and invention.

1938   Minnesota Mining and Manufacturing produces new reflective tape for traffic signs.

1939   Minnesota Mining and Manufacturing develops tape dispensers.

Archie builds and gives Edythe the Little Theater in St. Paul, Minnesota.

1940   Federal census shows Aunt Victoria Nason is still in the Bush household, plus Margot G. Smith, a maid, and Hildegarde A. Mortz, a maid.

1941   Minnesota Mining and Manufacturing is involved with products to support WW II.

1946   The company, Minnesota Mining and Manufacturing (3M), begins trading on the New York Stock Exchange.

1947   3M markets recording tape, ribbons and surgical tape.

1948   Archie is named Executive Vice President of 3M. The company produces hundreds of products.

1949   Archie is named chair of the Executive Committee of 3M.

1950   3M develops a fax copier.

1951   Thomas G. Bush dies and is buried in Granite Falls City Cemetery.

Archie and Edythe buy a home in Florida and they gradually take on significant roles in the community there, as they had in Minnesota. Archie buys and expands an orange ranch and invests in the cattle business.

3M is a global operation with offices in Australia,

Brazil, Canada, France, Germany, Mexico and the United Kingdom.

1953   Archie forms a philanthropic foundation bearing his last name. He launches his personal philanthropic efforts.

1954   3M advances recording tape for television.

1956   Archibald G. Bush receives an honorary doctorate degree from Hamline University in St. Paul, Minnesota.

1957   Reuben Bush dies October 29 and is buried in Granite Falls Hillcrest Cemetery.

A four mile long street in St. Paul, Minnesota, is renamed Bush Avenue, and runs to the 3M campus.

1958   Archie Bush returns to Granite Falls for a major celebration of his personal achievements and his generous help is providing land and bringing major new industry to the city. The street in front of the new development is named Bush Drive.

3M has a new product called Scotch Brite pads for cleaning.

1959   Archie celebrates 50 years with 3M.

1960   Half-sister Sadie Richardson dies and is buried in Granite Falls City Cemetery.

1961   3M continues to improve its hypoallergenic surgical tape and magnetic tape.

1962   3M opens its new world headquarters in Maplewood, Minnesota.

1963   Archie and Edythe both receive honorary degrees from Rollins College in Florida.

1966   Archibald Granville Bush dies at age 78 in Winter Park, Florida, on January 16 and is buried in Oakland Cemetery in St. Paul, Minnesota.

1968   Margaret Bush Hollensteiner dies and is buried in Granite Falls City Cemetery

1969   Minnie Bush dies and is buried in Granite Falls City Cemetery

1972   Edythe Bassler Bush dies and is buried in Oakland Cemetery in St. Paul, Minnesota

Resources

Resources used by Carl Narvestad:

Census records

Interviews

Brand of the Tartan: the 3M Story, by Virginia
    Huck, 1955, 1995

Newspapers

3M Megaphone, (company newsletter)

Local history sources in Renville, Chippewa and
    Yellow Medicine Counties

Courthouse records in these same counties, espe-
    cially land records

Plat maps for these same counties

Local and family photographs

Genealogy resources of the Valdres Samband

Personal knowledge from lifelong residence in the
    area, family connections

Interviews with Bush family members and others
    with direct and primary knowledge

Lutheran Church Records and histories

Renville County Histories

Yellow Medicine County Histories

Wang Township History monographs

Minneapolis Star and Tribune

St Paul Pioneer Press Post Dispatch

Granite Falls Advocate Tribune

Duluth News Tribune

Granite Falls City records

Resources used by Carol Heen:

Census and government records
Genealogy records
Internet research on Rollins College, Hamline
    University,
Minnesota Historical Society
Granite Falls Historical Society
New York Times
Orlando Sentinel
Minneapolis Star Tribune
St. Paul Pioneer Press Post Dispatch
3M websites
Bush Foundation website
Local history sources for Renville, Chippewa, and
    Yellow Medicine counties and Wang Township
Interviews: Paul and Barbara Benson, David
    Haroldson
Heen Digitization Project, Linda Heen
Ruth Slattum interview notes by Leslie Heen
Plat maps, Minnesota county and township maps
New Lisbon Post Office research and records
Valdres Norway farm histories in Bygdeboks
Carol L. Heen local history research, lectures,
    graduate and post-graduate writings
Lutheran Church records and histories
Granite Falls Advocate Tribune
Maynard Museum
Blegen Theodore. *Minnesota, A History of the State.*
    Minneapolis:University of Minnesota Press
    1963,1975.

Carley, Kenneth. *The Dakota War of 1862*. St. Paul: Minnesota Historical Society Press, 1961.

Curtiss-Wedge, Franklin. *The History of Renville County*. Chicago,: H.C. Cooper and Co, 1916.

Dahlin, Custis. *A History of the Dakota*. Roseville: Curtis A Dahlin, 2012.

Gilman, Rhoda, et al. *Red River Valley Trails*. St Paul: Minnesota Historical Society, 1979

Huck, Virginia. *Brand of the Tartan*: *The 3M Story*. New York: Appleton-Century-Crofts, 1955, 1995

Johnson, David W. *Hamline University, A history 1854-1994*. St. Paul: Regents of Hamline University, 1994

Jones, Evan. *The Minnesota*. New York: Holt Rinehart Winston, 1962.

Kaplan, Ziebarth, at al. *Minnesota Territory*. St. Paul:Minnesota Historical Society, 1999.

Lanegran David. *Minnesota on the Map*. St Paul: Minnesota Historical Society, 2008.

Narvestad Carl and Amy. *Granite Falls 1879-1979*. Granite Falls: Granite Falls Centennial Committee, 1979.

Narvestad, Carl and Amy. *A History of Yellow Medicine County, 1879 - 1979*

Narvestad, Carl and Amy. *History of Wang Township 1875-2000*. Granite Falls: Narvestad, 2000

Richland County Farmer Globe. *Ft. Abercrombie 1862*. Wahpeton, ND: Richland County Farmer Globe, 1936

White, Helen McCann. *Ho For the Goldfields*. St. Paul: Minnesota Historical Society, 1966

Wingerd Mary Lethert. *North Country*. St. Paul: University of Minnesota Press, 2010.

Carl and Amy Narvestad

Author, Carl T. Narvestad
1914-2003

Carl T. Narvestad was born and raised in Wang Township, south of Maynard, Minnesota. He promoted and loved local history, as evidenced by his many publications about the surrounding area. He coauthored many of these with his wife, Amy. Archie Bush's story was one he worked on for many years but never ascertained who would be interested in publishing the biography. He admired how a man from a small rural community could go on to build one of America's largest corporations due to his entrepreneurship. (Carl also strongly supported local businesses whose products and services became nationally and internationally known.) It is a great honor to have his work on this biography enhanced and finished.

– Kris Swanson, (Carl's stepdaughter)

Editor, Carol L. Heen, Ph.D.

Carol Heen holds advanced degrees from the University of Minnesota in Music History and American Studies. Her career has been in academic, arts and non-profit settings. A partner in Heen Century Farms, she has a deep commitment to local rural history, genealogy, and photo preservation.